Measurement of clinical performance

Practical approaches in acute myocardial infarction

Edited by

Robert West
Reader in Epidemiology
University of Wales College of Medicine, Cardiff

and

Robin Norris
Honorary Consultant Cardiologist
Clinical Effectiveness and Evaluation Unit
Royal College of Physicians

Clinical Effectiveness and Evaluation Unit
Royal College of Physicians

Faculty of Public Health Medicine

Acknowledgement

The Myocardial Infarction National Audit Project is funded by
the National Institute for Clinical Excellence

This publication is based on a conference held at the Royal College of Physicians
on 28 September 2000, organised jointly by the Clinical Effectiveness and
Evaluation Unit and the Royal College of Physicians and the Faculty of Public
Health Medicine.

Royal College of Physicians of London
11 St Andrews Place, London NW1 4LE
Registered Charity No. 210508

Faculty of Public Health Medicine
4 St Andrews Place
London NW1 4LB

Copyright © 2001 Royal College of Physicians of London
ISBN 1 86016 152 9

Cover design by Merriton Sharp
Typeset by Dan-Set Graphics, Telford, Shropshire
Printed in Great Britain by Sarum ColourView, Old Sarum, Salisbury

Foreword

The introduction of national service frameworks (NSFs) provided a renewed impetus to consider not only how to implement proposals to improve healthcare but to settle the even more important issue, do they work?

This publication, and the conference on which it is based, sets out to consider the practical approaches to measurement and to examine how we can meet the standards set by the NSF for coronary heart disease. It is intended and hoped that this could be a benchmark for the future approach to measurement in other NSFs. The reason for such optimism is based on the span of organisations supporting the conference and the breadth of expertise reflected in the contributors. Critical and controversial issues are considered, and also the more practical difficulties that exist both with respect to the limitations of some existing measures and with the problems of gathering data of a high quality.

In the past there has been an absence of appropriate and relevant information and of comprehensive measurements of the impact of such programmes. Many research projects and pioneering schemes have indicated possibilities but they have not always been followed up and developed.

It is particularly pleasing that the combined skills and approaches of clinical medicine and public health were brought together to address these issues. It is to be hoped that the interest and enthusiasm arising from the meeting and this subsequent publication will, together with the imperatives of an NSF agreement, ensure that not only is there service development but that this is accompanied by real progress in measurement. This will require further development of techniques of research and, perhaps more importantly, the publication and use of the results. This will be required at all levels and involve those providing care in planning the collection of information and dissemination locally and nationally. Health professionals, the public and politicians should have an interest in such a publication.

Professor Sir George Alberti   **Professor James McEwen**
President,   *President,*
Royal College of Physicians of London   *Faculty of Public Health Medicine*

December 2001

Contributors

Sir George Alberti
President, Royal College of Physicians, London

Raphael Balcon
Consultant Cardiologist, London Chest Hospital

John Birkhead
Associate Director, Clinical Effectiveness and Evaluation Unit, Royal College of Physicians, London

David Cunningham
Technical and Development Manager, Central Cardiac Audit Database

Iain Findlay
Consultant Physician and Cardiologist, Royal Alexandra Hospital, Paisley

Andrew Georgiou
Coronary Heart Disease Programme Co-ordinator, Clinical Effectiveness and Evaluation Unit, Royal College of Physicians, London

Rod Griffiths
Regional Director of Public Health, West Midlands Regional Office

Dame Deirdre Hine
Chairman, Commission for Health Improvement

Deborah Hughes
Cardiac Nurse Specialist, Torbay Hospital

Louise Knight
Project Co-ordinator Cardiology, Clinical Effectiveness and Evaluation Unit, Royal College of Physicians, London

Jonathan Mant
Senior Lecturer, Department of Primary Care and General Practice, University of Birmingham

Alastair Mason
Consultant Epidemiologist, National Centre for Health Outcomes Development, Oxford

James McEwen
President, Faculty of Public Health Medicine

Robin Norris
Honorary Consultant Cardiologist, Clinical Effectiveness and Evaluation Unit, Royal College of Physicians, London

Mike Pearson
Director, Clinical Effectiveness and Evaluation Unit, Royal College of Physicians, London

Anthony Rickards
Chairman, Central Cardiac Audit Database; Consultant Cardiologist, Royal Brompton Hospital, London

Lynne Walker
Project Co-ordinator Cardiology, Clinical Effectiveness and Evaluation Unit, Royal College of Physicians, London

Robert West
Reader in Epidemiology, University of Wales College of Medicine, Cardiff

Carol Westland
Service Manager, Central Cardiac Audit Database, Royal Brompton Hospital, London

Contents

Section One
General issues

Section Two

Issues specific to acute myocardial infarction

Introduction

Robert West and Robin Norris

The prime objective of clinical outcomes measurement is to monitor quality of care in order to ensure that the desired clinical outcomes are achieved in a satisfactory proportion of all patients treated. Monitoring of performance is necessary to establish that adequate standards are met in institutions (hospitals) and by individual professionals, and appropriate outcome measures are necessary to ensure that sensible and fair comparisons are possible. The final arbiters in evaluating performance in the treatment of episodes of acute medical illness are cure, discharge home and minimal long-term sequelae.

Thus, mortality inevitably emerges as an important clinical outcome indicator, but by no means the only important measure. Interest in analysis of outcome measurement in healthcare is not a recent phenomenon[1]. Several issues of measurement and interpretation of hospital statistics discussed at the Statistical Society of London over a century ago[2] are as relevant today.

This publication is based broadly on papers presented at a meeting sponsored jointly by the Royal College of Physicians (RCP) and the Faculty of Public Health Medicine, held at the RCP in September 2000. The purpose of the meeting and of this publication is to discuss the issues of performance measurement by bringing together the views and experience of practitioners from many different perspectives around the audit of acute myocardial infarction (AMI) as a practical example.

The selection of AMI as the subject of audit is not intended to be exclusive. It is presented primarily because of the importance of the disease, the evidence base for its treatment, recent developments in the audit of the treatment of AMI and the political and public interest in interhospital comparisons of outcome.

Many of the issues discussed are relevant in other areas of medicine, and many of the solutions considered or proposed have been considered or developed in other areas. However, ischaemic heart disease is the leading cause of death in most countries of the Western world and AMI is the leading cause of acute medical admissions in the UK. Thus, on the basis of patient numbers, measurement of performance in treatment of AMI is important. Mortality is high, particularly early after onset[3], so mortality features strongly as an outcome measure. Although some mortality following AMI may be inevitable and unavoidable, there are

1

many effective interventions which reduce mortality in both the short and longer term. This means that some portion of AMI 'case fatality' may be considered as 'avoidable mortality'[4], and that mortality may be regarded as a relevant measure of performance in audit of outcome[5].

The present era of audit of the treatment of AMI started in 1990 with formation of the Joint Audit Committee of the RCP and the British Cardiac Society. The effectiveness of thrombolytic treatment in reducing mortality had been evident in an overview of several early trials[6], and the importance of early administration had been demonstrated in the subsequent mega-trials[7,8]. Early thrombolytic treatment saves lives, so it behoves clinicians and hospitals to ensure that patients for whom thrombolysis is indicated, receive it. This is audit of process[5]. On formation of the joint committee, the first project to be started was an audit of 'door-to-needle' time[9-11].

What started as a collaborative project has now become a political imperative, following publication of the national service framework (NSF) for coronary heart disease[12]. Audit of the treatment of cardiac arrest before admission to hospital, the early delivery of thrombolytic treatment after arrival and the institution of secondary preventive measures on discharge are specifically required. As far as hospital treatment is concerned, the NSF priorities are thrombolytic treatment and secondary prevention.

However, early administration of a thrombolytic agent is not the only significant intervention in the early treatment of AMI. The benefits of early thrombolysis have been shown so conclusively in large trials that it is too easy to forget that treatment of ventricular fibrillation with the defibrillator saves many more lives than does thrombolysis[13,14]. Defibrillation, like the use of penicillin in pneumonia, has never been subjected to randomised clinical trials[15]. It is perhaps salutary to recognise that we have such large trials of thrombolytic treatment only because the benefit of thrombolysis by comparison is relatively modest. A full audit of AMI should therefore collect data on resuscitation and defibrillation in hospital. Moreover, the treatment of cardiac arrest outside hospital, introduced by Pantridge in Belfast[16] and by Chamberlain and his colleagues in Brighton[17], has extended the role of the ambulance service to that of a major player in the treatment of AMI. Audit of ambulance performance is therefore just as important as audit of process and outcomes in hospital, and is recognised as such by the NSF.

The first seven chapters in this publication discuss outcome measurement in general, from issues of quality in healthcare and professional and institutional performance (Hine), through the role of mortality as an outcome measure and considerations of its statistical analysis (West), with examples of how hospitals' league positions can be explained (Mason) and adjusted (Findlay), consideration of relative merits of measures of outcome and process (Mant), to discussion of how to influence or change professional practice (Griffiths). Finally, Pearson describes two previous clinical audits which led to the development of the Clinical Effectiveness and Evaluation Unit (CEEU) in the RCP.

The second series of seven chapters deals specifically with the Myocardial Infarction National Audit Project (MINAP) and includes the history of national audit of AMI leading up to MINAP (Birkhead), examples of the data recorded in MINAP (Cunningham, Rickards and Westland), the role of nurses in gathering these data (Hughes), proposals for audit of the vital pre-hospital phase of infarction (Norris) and discussion of the critical problems of maintaining data quality (Georgiou, Knight and Walker). The closing chapters discuss lessons which might be learned from recent regional audits of AMI (Norris), and possible future developments of MINAP to include invasive interventions and extensions from AMI to the acute ischaemic syndromes in general (Balcon).

We hope this publication will stimulate interest in clinical audit, which has been for too long a neglected and underperforming area of clinical and public health medicine.

References

1   Nightingale F. *Notes on hospitals*. London: J W Parker, 1859.
2   Statistical Society of London. Statistics of the general hospitals of London, 1861. *J Statist Soc London* 1862;**25**:384–8.
3   McNeilly RH, Pemberton J. Duration of last attack in 998 fatal cases of coronary artery disease and its relation to possible cardiac resuscitation. *Br Med J* 1968;**3**:139–42.
4   Holland W. Avoidable death as a measure of quality. *Qual Assur Health Care* 1990;**2**:227–33.
5   Donabedian A. Evaluating the quality of medical care. *Millbank Mem Fund Q* 1966;**44**(Suppl):166–206.
6   Stampfer MJ, Goldhaber SZ, Yusuf S, Peto R, Hennekens CH. Effect of intravenous streptokinase on acute myocardial infarction: pooled results from randomized trials. *N Engl J Med* 1982;**307**:1180–2.
7   Effectiveness of intravenous thrombolytic treatment in acute myocardial infarction. Gruppo Italiano per lo Studio della Streptochinasi nell'Infarto Miocardico (GISSI). *Lancet* 1986;**i**:397–402.
8   Randomised trial of intravenous streptokinase, oral aspirin, both, or neither among 17,187 cases of suspected acute myocardial infarction: ISIS-2. ISIS-2 (Second International Study of Infarct Survival) Collaborative Group. *Lancet* 1988;**ii**:349–60.
9   MacCallum AG, Stafford PJ, Jones C, Vincent R, *et al.* Reduction in hospital time to thrombolytic therapy by audit of policy guidelines. *Eur Heart J* 1990; **11**(Supp F):48–52.

10 Birkhead JS. Time delays in provision of thrombolytic treatment in six district hospitals. Joint Audit Committee of the British Cardiac Society and a Cardiology Committee of Royal College of Physicians of London. *Br Med J* 1992;**305**:445–8.

11 Birkhead JS. Thrombolytic treatment for myocardial infarction: an examination of practice in 39 United Kingdom hospitals. Myocardial Infarction Audit Group. *Heart* 1997;**78**:28–33.

12 Department of Health. *National service framework for coronary heart disease: modern standards and service models.* London: DoH, 2000.

13 Effect of time from onset to coming under care on fatality of patients with acute myocardial infarction: effect of resuscitation and thrombolytic treatment. The United Kingdom Heart Attack Study (UKHAS) Collaborative Group. *Heart* 1998;**80**:114–20.

14 Norris RM, on behalf of the Southern Heart Attack Response Project (SHARP). A new performance indicator for acute myocardial infarction. *Heart* 2001;**85**:395–401.

15 Julian DG, Norris RM. What constitutes evidence? A comparison of the impact of two therapies – one 'evidence-based', the other not – in the management of acute myocardial infarction. *Lancet* (in press).

16 Pantridge JF, Geddes JS. A mobile intensive care unit in the management of myocardial infarction. *Lancet* 1967;**ii**:271–3.

17 White NM, Parker WS, Binning RA, Kimber ER, *et al.* Mobile coronary care provided by ambulance personnel. *Br Med J* 1973;3:615–22.

Section One
General issues

1 | Clinical governance and the Commission for Health Improvement

Deirdre Hine

In this chapter I present an introduction to the Commission for Health Improvement (CHI)[1] and clinical governance and how these relate to the main subject of this book, the measurement of the clinical outcomes of care in acute myocardial infarction (AMI). I intend to focus on the first two topics because I know something about them. Also I suspect that both are still something of a mystery to many clinical colleagues. Finally, I would like to touch on the subject of whose outcomes we should be measuring.

The importance of clinical governance

First, I will attempt to explain why the concept of clinical governance and the establishment of CHI as a body to monitor the quality of care achieved through clinical governance were thought necessary. Some of us will recall the following passage from the Griffiths Report of 1983[2]:

> Rarely are precise management objectives set; there is little measurement of health output; clinical evaluation of particular practices is by no means common and economic evaluation of those practices extremely rare. Nor can the NHS display a ready assessment of the effectiveness with which it is meeting the needs of the people it serves.

Can we, over a decade later, say with hand on heart that things have radically changed?

I was not privy to the thinking which led to the concept of clinical governance or to the views of CHI on this before undertaking the chairmanship of the Commission. However, it seems to me that there was a general perception that widespread variation still existed both in protocols for treatment and in standards of clinical care generally, despite the introduction of medical audit, clinical audit, the evidence-based medicine movement and the initiatives to ensure clinical effectiveness. Also, that such variation in performance was persisting despite growing research-based evidence of the effectiveness of some interventions and the lack of effectiveness of others.

Secondly, it was felt that some new mechanism for assuring the quality of care was necessary to restore public confidence in the wake of a series of high profile service failures.

Thirdly, and to me most importantly, there was recognition of a need to redress the balance from the focus which for the past decade had been on costs and efficiency in the NHS to one of quality and effectiveness: thus, the new statutory duty of boards and chief executives to account not only for their financial stewardship but also for the quality of the care given to their patients.

Clinical governance therefore requires NHS organisations to set up and demonstrate a systematic approach to improving clinical care. The concept was formalised in law by the Health Act 1999 and by the responsibilities laid on the whole board of a hospital, health authority or primary care group. To those of us who had sat on NHS bodies, from trust boards to health authorities and as health department executives, and who over many years had felt frustrated at the attention given to finance on the agenda of such bodies at the expense of attention to care of patients, this rebalancing of accountabilities seemed to offer enormous opportunities to address our concerns.

What is clinical governance?

Clinical governance recognises that achieving quality in healthcare is a complex and highly sophisticated exercise. In essence, it is the systematic co-ordination of all the elements that contribute to improving quality. It includes:

- risk management
- clinical audit to ensure that clinical care is up to date and effective
- processes for ensuring that staff have access to and use professional education training and development opportunities
- mechanisms for ensuring appropriate supervision of staff
- systems which ensure that adverse incidents and near misses are reported, recorded and learned from and, not least,
- the ways used to ensure the involvement of patients and their families in informed decisions on their individual care and on the way in which services are organised and developed for them.

The Commission for Health Improvement

It was quickly recognised that, as with medical and clinical audit, the introduction of this new accountability and its implementation would be likely to be difficult and that if its implementation was patchy, as with those previous initiatives, it might lead to even greater disparity in the quality of care offered by different institutions. Thus, CHI was set up as a body which would monitor and report on the success of the NHS in absorbing and delivering this new accountability.

CHI is a statutory independent body covering England and Wales, working with other organisations and with the NHS itself to achieve the aim of demonstrable improvement. Clearly, one facet of that demonstrable improvement must be improved clinical outcomes, so the way in which outcomes can be consistently and accurately measured is extremely important to CHI.

CHI is still a young organisation, but already aware of the monumental and highly sensitive task which lies ahead. We have developed the following six principles to guide our work, that it should be:

1 Patient centred.
2 Independent and fair.
3 Developmental, supporting learning.
4 Evidence-based.
5 Open and accessible.
6 Providing the same continuous improvement expectation of ourselves that we apply to others.

I would single out three of these in particular.

Patient centredness

The patient's experience will always be the touchstone of our work and the basis of our report. By patient experience, I do not mean solely satisfaction, but the whole outcome of care as evidenced by clear objective evidence of the effectiveness of clinical interventions, and also by the extent to which patients feel that the cost of those interventions to *them* in terms of inconvenience, discomfort, distress, pain or additional anxiety has been justified by the improvement in their functional status and/or their sense of well-being.

Developmental, supporting learning

We also intend, as far as possible, to be developmental rather than judgemental in our work. It has always seemed to me that holding up a mirror in which those undertaking care can recognise how far they are or are not achieving their own aims is more likely to stimulate them to improvement than is an approach of naming and shaming.

Evidence-based

As far as is humanly possible within the constraints of admittedly underdeveloped current information systems, the intention is that our assessments will be evidenced-based.

Statutory functions of the Commission for Health Improvement

CHI is required to achieve its aim through its four statutory functions:

1 Reviews of clinical governance in all NHS institutions at least once every four years, thus contributing to continuous quality improvement locally.

2 The conduct of national studies into the implementation and impact of national service frameworks (NSFs) as these are rolled out by the Department of Health together with the guidance and guidelines devised for use within those frameworks.

3 Undertaking investigations into institutions in which there have been serious or persistent clinical failures.

4 Providing advice and guidance, as time goes on, on the development of clinical governance itself.

I will now discuss clinical governance reviews and national studies in slightly more detail, and touch on the role that outcomes measurement and outcomes monitoring will play within these.

Clinical governance reviews

The reviews will provide an independent assessment of systems to assure quality of care and improvement in individual NHS units. It is intended that they will be developmental for the organisations reviewed, and also provide an independent assessment of their quality for the local community and for patients using these services. It is our endeavour to make them fair and consistent in their judgements across all institutions in England and Wales. The review process will focus on three levels:

▮ patients

▮ clinical teams, and

▮ corporate organisation.

As already indicated, patients and their experiences will be at the root of our assessment. However, we will also look at clinical teams, examining:

▮ their mechanisms for assessing their own outcomes (ie clinical audit)

- their communications with patients
- how they share good practice, and
- how they learn from others.

At the corporate level, we want to ensure not only that a corporate strategy for continuous improvement exists but also that the board is making sure that it is understood and applied throughout the organisation, setting the culture for achieving excellence from the top, taking full responsibility for quality of care as well as financial probity.

Our assessments will be essentially peer reviews because we will ensure that practising clinicians are always part of the review team make-up. However, they will recognise that patients are *partners* in care by also including lay people in every team.

Evidence gathering

The first stage of clinical governance reviews will be evidence gathering about the unit (initially an acute hospital) being reviewed. It will include analysis of published performance indicators together with other data provided by the hospital. This will always include a standardised self-assessment document compiled by the organisation itself, and might include any locally produced outcomes information, reports of Royal College inspections, etc. At this stage, there will also be meetings with local stakeholders to gather their views. Local general practitioners, patients' associations, the community health council and members of the general public will be invited to give their assessment of the quality of care – both good and not so good!

Aspects of clinical governance to be reviewed

Using this indicative data and information, the review team – which will be multidisciplinary, always including medical, nursing and lay members – will decide on the specific aspects of clinical governance they will examine. At the clinical team level, they will focus on up to four individual teams, which inevitably in some hospitals will include cardiac services including care of AMI patients. The aim will be to look at the less successful services and teams and to hold up a mirror to their organisation to try to identify where there are opportunities for improvement. They will also look at the successful services and teams within an organisation to highlight and encourage sharing of best practice. It is true that there is sometimes no need for less successful teams to look any further than at other parts of their own organisations – yet they often do not do this.

In this way, we will be providing honest views to the local population about the quality of care that their local hospital gives, but also proving to them that the hospital includes thriving areas of excellence. There will be opportunities for staff, including clinicians, to meet with and talk to the team if they wish, on a confidential basis if appropriate. Reports of the reviews will go to the organisation concerned, but will also be made publicly available within the catchment area of the service and published on our website.

Quality of care across boundaries

In addition to assessing clinical governance *within* organisations, there is clearly a need to assess the quality of care *across* organisations and boundaries. For this reason, one of the main features of the government's quality framework is the setting of standards and guidelines to be delivered locally and to be monitored through a number of mechanisms including CHI.

National studies

Our first national study is an 18-month study of the review of the implementation of the Calman-Hine report[3]. This was not an NSF, though it was a precursor of those to come later. We are currently in the data collection stage of this study; this will be followed by sampling organisations and processes across regions following patient pathways for cancer.

We will eventually be undertaking a national study of the implementation of the NSF for coronary heart disease, issued in March 2000[4]. Clearly, the service needs time to study, absorb and have the chance to implement the framework before it would be useful to look at its implementation. Standards 5, 6 and 7 in the standards table relate particularly to the care of victims of heart attacks and other acute coronary syndromes. Standard 7 specifically states that trusts should put in place agreed protocols/systems of care so that people admitted to hospital with proven heart attack are appropriately assessed and offered treatments of proven clinical and cost-effectiveness to reduce their risk of disability and death. I foresee that standard 7 will be a key to our work when we begin to undertake our study of this NSF and the extent to which clinical governance has or has not contributed to its implementation.

Investigations

I will only briefly discuss CHI investigations. However, I want to emphasise what is not generally understood, that our investigations are *not* about individuals, about one-off complaints – not even into the incidents which have caused concern – and we certainly do not have the power to remove staff as a result of our investigations. The investigations are mainly directed to exploring system failures and how the index event or series of events was able to happen and was not prevented by robust clinical systems. Our aim within these investigations will be to draw a line under what has often been an unhappy episode for a trust, which in some cases has already involved disciplinary action, and to make recommendations about these syndromes to minimise the chance of recurrence of harm to patients.

CHI's starting point is always the patient's experience. This also applies to outcomes. I want to re-emphasise that there are two sides to outcomes. CHI is particularly interested in the outcome as seen from the patient's point of view. The final test is whether the patient thinks it has all been worth it:

The patient's point of view: the patient's assessment of whether:

▪ they feel they have benefited sufficiently, taking into account the inconvenience, discomfort and so on

▪ the disadvantages were equally balanced by the improvements gained, and

▪ they were treated with compassion and dignity.

Clinical outcomes: the other part is hard clinical outcomes, which are based on reliable comparative outcome measures.

CHI is looking for a balance between the two. The former is not always easy to measure and is always subjective. In our clinical governance reviews, techniques such as patient diaries are used, while in the national studies patient focus groups will be used as an information gathering method. However, only clinicians can assist us in defining the criteria and pointers that should be looked at in terms of clinical outcomes.

Clinical indicators

We are aware of the difficulty in defining such indicators and the fact that, though a small number could be clearly defined as a result of the work which led to the Myocardial Infarction National Audit Project (MINAP), many others were felt to be difficult to capture with current information systems and/or impossible to tie down sufficiently to make them meaningful. It is tempting, therefore, to say that we cannot use outcome measures until they have been perfected. I suggest that unless clinical teams continue with their efforts to audit their performance against agreed outcome measures, we will not move forward at all, and that unless CHI includes in its work the use of such outcome measures as have been agreed, further improvement will not be stimulated.

Published clinical indicators (eg in-hospital deaths within 30 days of admission with AMI) may be crude and liable to be misunderstood and misinterpreted if not used carefully, especially if used within league tables. They are not perfect but, as we are all well aware, perfect indicators do not currently exist.

CHI will always look at these indicators when doing clinical governance reviews, but they will be used as one tool, not in isolation, to make final judgements. However, a word of warning: where a trust has a high indicator value, we will expect them to know that and to understand and be able to explain why and what they are doing about it. Clinicians must be at the forefront of this measuring process. They know better than anyone what to look for. Perhaps more importantly, if the medical profession does not do it, others will do it for them.

The future

The Commission for Health Improvement is still in the early stages of its development. Our first four pilot clinical governance review reports and our first two investigation reports have recently been published[5,6]. I would like to present the advent of the CHI as an opportunity rather than a threat to clinical freedom. Our task is not to seek out the incompetent, let alone the bad apples, within the NHS. We all know that they are extremely rare. We are also aware that in today's climate anything less than perfection in clinical care is not easily forgiven by the general public – yet doctors, nurses and other clinical staff are only human. Against this, stakes are extremely high. If clinicians make a mistake, the consequences can be potentially fatal or disabling.

The members of my Commission recognise that all clinicians want to do their best for their patients. However, neither clinicians nor CHI will be able to demonstrate that they are achieving that best unless we can both assess and understand their clinical outcomes. We are particularly concerned to invite clinicians to work with us in partnership. We are very aware that our methodologies must be developed as we accumulate more and more experience in using them.

References

1   *The Health Act*, Section 19. London: The Stationery Office, 1999.
2   Department of Health and Social Security. *NHS Management Inquiry (Griffiths Report)*. London: DHSS, 1983:10.

3   Calman K, Hine D. *A policy framework for commissioning cancer services: guidance for purchasers and providers of cancer services.* Report by the Expert Advisory Group on Cancer. London: Department of Health, Welsh Office, 1995.

4   Department of Health. *National service framework for coronary heart disease: modern standards and service models.* London: DoH, 2000.

5   Commission for Health Improvement. *Report of a clinical governance review at Southampton University Hospitals NHS Trust.* London: CHI, 2000.

6   Commission for Health Improvement. *Investigation into Carmarthenshire NHS Trust.* London: CHI, 2000.

2 | Performance indicators and mortality league tables

Robert West

The most stringent tests of performance lie with measurement of outcome and in acute medicine the measurement of mortality. There has been a long history of analysis and thoughtful interpretation of hospital mortality statistics[1], yet many overly naïve presentations still prevail. Before discussing uses and abuses of mortality league tables it is appropriate briefly to consider why mortality tends to head the list of performance indicators. The principal reasons are that mortality is the most severe test of effectiveness or ineffectiveness; there is little ambiguity over recognition of the fact of death, although there may be less certainty over the classification of its cause[2]. Other important reasons for mortality following acute myocardial infarction (AMI) being listed amongst the initial set of NHS performance indicators to include mortality[3] are, first, AMI is the most common cause of acute medical admission and, secondly, case fatality rates are relatively high by comparison with many other conditions. However, mortality is not the only measure, and mortality alone would be insensitive for much of clinical practice[4].

Hospital mortality data

Hospital mortality data are useful as a measure of quality of care – perhaps the ultimate measure of quality, since many medical interventions are directed at preventing death or, perhaps more correctly, *postponing* death for the major chronic diseases like heart disease and cancer. When death is preventable, hospital mortality data may be compared against an absolute standard. More commonly, and in the example of AMI when some death is inevitable, comparison may be made with a 'standard' or with other hospitals. Higher than expected death rates may then be indication of:

▪ deficiencies in provision
▪ poor clinical management
▪ problems with supporting services, or
▪ weaknesses in communication.

When the problems have been identified, audit of hospital mortality allows monitoring of progress towards best practice or achieving an agreed standard[5].

Evidence-based medicine

In the era of 'evidence-based' medicine[6] these standards evolve from a long hierarchy of evidence, from basic science and laboratory research, through primary clinical trials and multicentre randomised controlled trials to the synthesis of primary evidence in systematic reviews (including statistical overviews or 'meta-analysis'). There is now a widely held belief that there is so much primary research that professional reviewers are needed to sift through the wealth of sometimes conflicting evidence[7,8].

Guidelines

The accumulated evidence, aided by thorough systematic reviews when they exist, is summarised into clinical and service guidelines, usually by specialist professional groups under the auspices of, for example, the Royal Colleges[9]. Important arguments for guidelines are the rates of advancement in science and of change of evidence that lead to textbooks, the former source of reviewed knowledge, being out of date. The rate of change of evidence is recognised in many guidelines, which suggest dates for their own review or replacement. Guidelines, in turn, can become incorporated into standards by both healthcare 'providers' and health service 'commissioners', as for example in the national service framework for coronary heart disease[10]. Once standards are set, they can be policed by bodies like the Commission for Health Improvement (see Chapter 1).

Abuses of hospital data

Abuses of performance indicators, in particular of ranking on one outcome measure, as in the league tables of hospital mortality, lie primarily with victimisation of the professions and scapegoating individuals, and with alarming patients or the public as potential patients. Although, through the 'purchaser/provider' split, the NHS moved some years ago to a quasi-market, urgently admitted patients rarely exercise choice and, with evidence-based emphasis on urgency, general practitioners rarely exercise choice on behalf of AMI patients.

The abuse of hospital mortality data, and of statistics generally, arises through inadequate analysis, misunderstanding and misinterpretation[11]. Some of the leading contributions to misrecording and inadequate analysis of case fatality rates are briefly illustrated by the example of 30-day mortality of AMI patients in 18 Welsh hospitals (Fig 1)[12]. The figure (with 95% confidence intervals (CI)) shows one hospital with in-hospital mortality statistically significantly above the Welsh average, one below and two each almost significantly above or below.

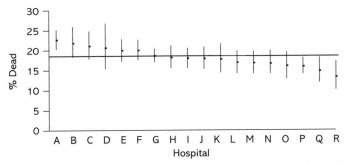

Fig 1. Deaths in hospital within 30 days of emergency admission with acute myocardial infarction: age standardised rate with 95% confidence intervals. (*Note:* these indicators are not a definitive measure of clinical effectiveness but should be used alongside other information as a starting point for discussion and further investigation.)

The denominator

Some epidemiological principles to consider in the measurement of a rate include:

- diagnosis/definition
- coding
- counting
- accuracy
- completeness, and
- lack of bias.

Diagnosis/definition

Under diagnosis, it is necessary to consider the definition of AMI, and whether or not some angina or even non-cardiac chest pain may be included. A recent proposal[13] to replace the World Health Organization (WHO) classification with measurement of troponin illustrates this point. It is also necessary to employ uniform criteria over inclusion of AMI secondary to some other condition or inclusion only of primary AMI as the principal diagnosis leading to admission.

Coding

The same considerations apply to coding, but in most hospital record systems this is a separate stage in the recording process undertaken by coding clerks. The WHO European Monitoring Trends and Determinants in Cardiovascular Disease (MONICA) project has shown that, even in exemplary studies, interpretation of diagnostic criteria, inclusion/ exclusion guidelines and coding rules can vary between study centres[14].

Counting

Another feature of counting that affects the denominator is definition of 'admission' or 'episode'. After many years of counting admissions (and discharges and deaths), the NHS moved to the 'finished consultant episode' – a wonderfully manipulable denominator. Hospitals with more consultants in more specialties have more opportunity of transferring patients between themselves to chalk up more episodes, which may raise hospital revenue as well as lower hospital death rates. Recent analyses of hospital death rates have found it necessary to recreate 'admission' by selecting only those 'episodes' that lead to death or discharge[15].

Lastly, in counting the denominator, particularly for conditions with high early mortality like AMI, clear guidelines are necessary for the exclusion (or inclusion) of patients who die on arrival. The classification 'brought in dead' is well recognised in accident and emergency departments but, with the present emphasis on speed of transfer to hospital possibly following early resuscitation by paramedics, a new classification of 'brought in nearly dead' may become a feature of AMI audit. There is an interesting play off here between the performance indicators of ambulance services and receiving hospitals.

Accuracy, completeness and lack of bias

In all the above there is need for accuracy, completeness and absence of systematic bias in interpretations of the rules between hospitals to ensure that comparable data are compared. Several studies of routine data have revealed major gaps and inaccuracies. The Department of Health itself left a gap of over two years between the end of hospitals activity analysis and the beginning of hospital episode statistics (HES) and allowed considerable confusion over 'episodes' and 'spells' in the early years of HES.

The numerator

Having recorded the denominator in a uniform and fair manner, it is necessary to establish uniform and fair rules for recording the numerator. The routine data for England and Wales remain weaker in this respect than the Scottish because the former are based on 'hospital deaths'. The HES and patient episode database for Wales systems are able to provide only 'hospital deaths/episodes' or selected subsets of these (eg 'hospital deaths within 30 days/episodes leading to discharge or death')[15]. Record linkage is necessary to include deaths following discharge. Fairer mortality comparisons would be based on 30-day mortality, which included community deaths[16,17].

Statistical adjustments

Age and sex. Statistical adjustments are logical and potentially important so that 'like is compared with like'. The most common adjustments or standardisations are for age and sex, as for the well-known standardised mortality ratio (SMR). The Welsh data illustrated in Fig 1 were standardised for age but an interesting observation was that, depending on the method of age standardisation or age standard chosen, three different hospitals could have been labelled as recording the highest mortality.

Other adjustments. Further adjustments may be undertaken to include:

▪ history (eg previous AMI or coronary revascularisation)

▪ co-morbidity (eg diabetes)

▪ other primary cause (eg generalised organ failure, with AMI one among many)

▪ potential explanatory variables or characteristics, such as ethnic group or holiday visitor, which might affect the mortality of one or two hospitals while having little effect on mortality in the majority

▪ 'case-mix', which can change the death rate and hence the ranking – but, with a common disease like AMI that is almost routinely admitted, and when hospitals in the comparison accept the full unselected case-mix from their catchment populations, adjustments for case-mix often make relatively little difference because each hospital admits poor risk and high risk patients in comparable proportions.

Other statistical considerations

Several further statistical considerations are relevant to the fair presentation and interpretation of hospital mortality data.

Sample size. For many conditions, hospital death rates are based on quite small numbers and therefore the precision of the estimates is poor. Statisticians have encouraged the use of 95% CIs about point estimates (as in Fig 1). A point not so widely appreciated is that the ranks in the league table are also point estimates (of rank) and derived from the same data as the (standardised) death rates and with the same degree of imprecision. In presenting comparative data on mortality following cardiac surgery in the USA, Goldstein and Spiegelhalter proposed 95% CIs on ranks[18]. In the illustration of AMI mortality in 18 Welsh hospitals, CIs of the ranks would suggest that only three of the hospitals might *not* have been at the top of the league table with the lowest mortality.

Time variation and 'regression to the mean'. Another familiar consideration is variation in time. A simple practical approach to this would be to repeat the measure after one year to see whether the hospital that performs badly this year performs badly again the following year. However, clinicians, managers and politicians might be unhappy with such 'wait and see' solutions: if there is a problem and a reason is found for the poor performance, they will wish to see the problem addressed *now* and performance improved before next year's statistics are analysed.

This variation in time effect can be estimated using a statistical technique called 'shrinkage', which estimates this time effect without waiting for the accumulation of many years of data to accumulate[18]. It is similar to 'regression to the mean'. A clinical analogy might be measurement of blood pressure and classification of hypertension. Single casual measurements in many individuals in a population provide a good idea of the relationship between blood pressure and cardiovascular risk, but a single blood pressure measurement may not define hypertension in an individual. More measurements per individual usually show that the average individual's blood pressure is nearer to the population mean than was the original measurement – hence 'regression to the mean'. Few clinicians would label an individual hypertensive, and condemn him or her to a lifetime of antihypertensive treatment, on the basis of one blood pressure measurement. It might be similarly irrational to label a hospital as having unacceptably high AMI mortality rates on the basis of one year's data. The average of a hospital's mortality statistics is likely to be closer to the population mean than the first casual measurement. Thus, if the measure were to be repeated a number of times, outliers would be expected to provide averages closer to the population mean. This is what 'shrinkage' estimates.

Clinicians, managers, the public and the media must be educated to recognise that a simple, single figure rank in a league table is a gross simplification and that there is rarely one 'bottom of the league' hospital.

Discussion of the findings

However, having acknowledged all the above, it remains possible that there are underperforming hospitals with statistically significantly high death rates after all appropriate adjustments. It is important to acknowledge the role of full, frank and open discussions of the findings and of the possible underlying problem[4,5]. Without such discussion, the problem – if there be a problem – may remain unresolved.

An audit of coronary artery bypass surgery in New Zealand many years ago serves to illustrate the importance of full examination of the data and open discussion of their interpretation. This audit headed off what might have escalated into a 'Bristol situation'[19]. There may be a simple explanation, or the statistics may still misrepresent the situation: for example, there may still be a confounder not taken into account in the adjustments. In few biological associations is as much as half the variance explained by known risk factors, which means that half remains unexplained. Full analysis of the data and thorough examination of possible explanations will usually lead to improvements in patient care which (as we should need no reminding) is the objective of auditing these important outcome measures.

References

1   Statistical Society of London. Statistics of the general hospitals of London 1861. *J Statist Soc Lond* 1862;**25**:384–8.

2   Haesman MA, Lipworth L. *Accuracy of certification of cause of death.* London: Her Majesty's Stationery Office, 1966.

3   Department of Health. *The NHS performance guide 1994–5: raising the standard.* Leeds: DoH, 1995.

4   Nightingale F. *Hospital statistics. International Statistics Congress.* London: Eyre and Spottiswoode, 1860.

5   Codman EA. *A study in hospital efficiency as demonstrated by the case reports of the first five years of a private hospital.* Boston: Todd, 1916.

6   Sackett DL, Haynes RB, Guyatt GH, Tugwell P. *Clinical epidemiology: a basic science for clinical medicine.* Boston: Little Brown, 1991.

7   Sackett D (ed). *The Cochrane Collaboration in Cochrane Collaboration Handbook.* Oxford: NHS R & D, 1994.

8   Sheldon T, Chalmers I. The UK Cochrane Centre and the NHS Centre for reviews and dissemination: respective roles within the information systems strategy of the NHS R&D programme, coordination and principles underlying collaboration. *Health Econ* 1994;**3**:201–3.

9   Guideline for the management of patients with acute coronary syndromes without persistent ECG ST segment elevation. British Cardiac Society Guidelines and Medical Practice Committee and Royal College of Physicians Clinical Effectiveness and Evaluation Unit. *Heart* 2001;**85**:133–42.

10   Department of Health. *National service framework for coronary heart disease: modern standards and service models.* London: DoH, 2000.

11   West RR. Interpreting government statistics on acute hospital care *Br Med J* 1987;**295**:509–10.

12   *Clinical indicators for the NHS 1995–1998.* Cardiff: Welsh Office, 1999.

13   Myocardial infarction redefined – a consensus document of The Joint European Society of Cardiology/American College of Cardiology Committee for

the redefinition of myocardial infarction. Review. *Eur Heart J* 2000;**21**: 1502–13.

14 Tunstall-Pedoe H, Kuulasmaa K, Amouyel P, Arveiler D, *et al.* Myocardial infarction and coronary deaths in the World Health Organization MONICA Project. Registration procedures, event rates, and case-fatality rates in 38 populations from 21 countries in four continents. *Circulation* 1994;**90**:583–612.

15 Jarman B, Gault S, Alves B, Hider A, *et al.* Explaining differences in English hospital death rates using routinely collected data. *Br Med J* 1999;**318**: 1515–20.

16 Capewell S, Kendrick S, Boyd J, Cohen G, *et al.* Measuring outcomes: one month survival after acute myocardial infarction in Scotland. *Heart* 1996;**76**:70–5.

17 Birkhead J, Goldacre M, Mason A, Wilkinson E, *et al* (eds). Health outcome indicators, myocardial infarction: report of a working group to the Department of Health. Oxford: National Centre for Health Outcomes Development, 1999.

18 Goldstein H, Spiegelhalter D. League tables and their limitations: statistical issues in comparisons of institutional performance. *J Roy Stat Soc* 1996;**159**:385–443.

19 West RR, Willis JD. An example of medical audit under political pressure. *Int J Epidemiol* 1983;**12**:482–6.

3 | Comparative outcome indicators for acute myocardial infarction

Alastair Mason

Ideal health outcome indicators

In the mid-1990s the Department of Health commissioned the National Centre for Health Outcomes Development (NCHOD) to develop ideal comparative health outcome indicators for 10 clinical conditions, one of which was acute myocardial infarction (AMI). Ideal indicators were defined as what should be known, and realistically could be known, about the condition being addressed. Thus, the work was not constrained by existing data sets, and could take into account information developments such as the introduction of the new NHS number.

The overall aim was to recommend a comprehensive menu of indicators. A standard approach was taken for all the conditions addressed. A broadly based multidisciplinary working group for each condition, comprising clinicians, managers and representatives of patients' and research interests, was responsible for overseeing the work. Crucial to the success of the enterprise was the development of a comprehensive health outcome model that formed the basis for choosing a set of candidate outcome indicators. A full data specification was drafted for each of the candidate indicators shown in Table 1.

The NCHOD report, published in 1999[1], has been an important input into the development of the various indicators associated with the national service framework (NSF) for coronary heart disease[2] and the work by the Royal College of Physicians on a minimum data set for auditing AMI[3].

NCHOD has continued to develop since the publication of the reports and to refine the candidate outcome indicators for the 10 conditions studied. In particular, using the Oxford Record Linkage System (ORLS) database, detailed work has been done on reviewing the methods of:

- calculation of admission and re-admission rates
- population-based mortality, and
- case fatality rates.

The main issues being addressed in this work are shown in Table 2.

ORLS was started in 1962; since 1985 it has covered a population of 2.5 million people living in the former Oxford Region. The data

Table 1. Candidate health outcome indicators for acute myocardial infarction (AMI).

Health outcome indicator	Measure
Population-based	▪ AMI rate ▪ Mortality from AMI
Relating to CHD risk factors	▪ Proportion of a population who report ceasing smoking in the year ▪ Mean systolic BP in a population over 16 years of age ▪ Proportion of hypertensive patients with latest systolic below 160 mmHg ▪ Proportion of a population identified as at high risk of CHD ▪ Summary of changes in a population of CHD risk
Relating to management of AMI	▪ Admission rate for all/first-ever AMI ▪ Re-admission rate within a year for AMI/any CVS event ▪ Case fatality rate at 30 days/one year ▪ Proportion of admissions for AMI receiving thrombolysis ▪ Timings: onset of symptoms/call for help/arrive hospital/thrombolysis ▪ Timings: call for help/availability of defibrillation
Measured six months after first-ever AMI	▪ Level of risk for CHD ▪ Impact of symptoms on function ▪ Assessment of health status/quality of life

BP = blood pressure; CHD= coronary heart disease; CVS = cardiovascular system.

comprise hospital episodes person-linked with each other and with birth and mortality details.

Case fatality rates

The case fatality rate (CFR) has long been recognised as potentially a most useful measure for comparing the ability of organisations to manage AMI. However, this indicator can be calculated in several different ways, and how it is done may significantly alter a hospital's position in any case fatality league table.

Recently, NCHOD has investigated the effect of time interval to death, location of death and methods of death recording on hospital CFR comparisons. The data analysed were for about 18,000 admissions in 1994–1998 with AMI listed anywhere on the admission record for the eight main hospitals involved in ORLS. Case fatality rates for different time periods and location of death were calculated. In the initial analyses shown in this chapter these were:

▪ in-hospital

▪ 30-day anywhere

▪ 90-day anywhere, and

▪ 365-day anywhere.

Table 2. Issues relevant to compiling indicators derived from linked data.

Relevant issue	Options available
Related to initial/only admission when used in calculating the indicators	▪ Completed consultant episodes or continuous inpatient spells ▪ Emergency, elective or all admissions ▪ Diagnostic codes to be included ▪ Primary diagnosis only or diagnosis anywhere on the clinical record
Related to admission rates	▪ Event-based or person-based rates
Related to population mortality and case fatality rates	▪ Diagnostic coding, condition-specific or all causes ▪ Diagnostic coding, underlying cause or anywhere on certificate ▪ Location of death, in hospital or anywhere ▪ Time interval from start of initial admission to death
Related to re-admission rates	▪ Completed consultant episodes or continuous inpatient spells ▪ Emergency or all re-admissions ▪ Time interval from end of initial admission and start of re-admission ▪ Exclusion of initial admissions ending in early death within time frame ▪ Accounting for transfers between hospitals
General points	▪ Age/sex and other standardisation ▪ Statistical power, adequate numbers to show differences ▪ Methodology used for linking and completeness of matching ▪ Accuracy and completeness of data

Case fatality rates were also calculated using different methods of recording death. For each time interval, CFRs were derived for deaths from:

▪ all causes after AMI

▪ AMI when it was recorded as the underlying cause of death, and

▪ AMI when it was recorded anywhere on the death certificate.

To enable comparisons, multiple logistic regression modelling was used to adjust for age group and sex, and for each set of CFRs a resultant odds ratio (OR) was calculated for each hospital with respect to reference hospital B.

Table 3 shows the effect on the comparative positions of the eight hospitals when CFRs were calculated taking death from all causes and using four different time interval/location of death combinations.

Table 3. Effect of death location/time interval on hospital rankings. Odds ratios (OR) relative to hospital B, all causes of death. (ORs in italics and bold are significant at the 1% and 0.1% levels, respectively.)

Hospital	Death in hospital	Death anywhere at:		
		30 days	90 days	365 days
A	<u>0.44</u>	0.97	0.97	0.98
B	1.00	1.00	1.00	1.00
C	1.01	1.03	1.04	1.13
D	1.06	1.06	1.09	1.10
E	1.10	1.15	*1.20*	*1.23*
F	1.18	1.20	1.16	1.24
G	*1.35*	*1.35*	*1.32*	1.20
H	**<u>1.37</u>**	**<u>1.37</u>**	**<u>1.41</u>**	**<u>1.30</u>**

Results of case fatality measurements

The results were the following:

▪ *Hospital A* has an amazingly low in-hospital CFR, but does not differ significantly from reference *hospital B* for the other measures. Further investigation has shown that this low figure is not due to superlative management of AMI but it is a spurious result due to data coding problems.

▪ Of the bottom four hospitals, *hospital E* is significantly different (at the 1% level) for the 90- and 365-day 'death anywhere' measures.

▪ Although *hospital F* has an OR higher than *hospital E* for three of the four measures, it is not significantly different from the reference hospital for any measure.

▪ *Hospital G* is significantly different (at the 1% level) for three measures.

▪ *Hospital H* is significantly different (at the 0.1% level) for all the measures.

Table 4 shows the effect of calculating CFRs with the three different ways of recording cause of death, with death recorded as occurring anywhere within 30 days. The results for the three methods of calculation are the following:

▪ *Based on all causes of death after AMI admission*: G (at 1% level) and H (at the 0.1% level) are statistically different from reference hospital B.

▪ *Based on AMI recorded anywhere on the death certificate*: E and F (at the 1% level) and G and H (at the 0.1% level) are significantly different.

Table 4. Effect of recording of cause of death on hospital rankings. Odds ratio (OR) relative to hospital B, 30-day mortality. (ORs in italics and bold are significant at the 1% and 0.1% levels, respectively.)

Hospital	All causes	Acute myocardial infarction	
		Any mention	Underlying cause
A	0.97	0.95	1.00
B	1.00	1.00	1.00
C	1.03	1.11	1.14
D	1.10	1.13	1.15
E	1.15	*1.27*	**1.32**
F	1.20	*1.22*	*1.33*
G	*1.35*	**1.46**	**1.54**
H	**1.37**	**1.51**	**1.50**

▮ *Based on AMI as the underlying cause.* F (at the 1% level) and E, G and H (at the 0.1% level) are significantly different.

Deaths in hospital not recorded on a patient admission system

In the NCHOD health outcome indicators report[1] it was noted that the derivation of mortality rates for AMI has complications not generally shared by other conditions. Many patients with AMI die before reaching hospital or in the accident and emergency department before they can be registered on a patient administration system (PAS). AMI is also responsible for most sudden deaths occurring outside hospital.

NCHOD are currently engaged in a major study to identify whether population-based mortality rates and CFRs are altered significantly when their derivation includes deaths on hospital premises not recorded on a PAS and sudden deaths occurring outside hospital. Early results show that these factors may make a major difference to CFRs, and consequently to the position of hospitals in any league tables based on them.

Conclusion

If the government wish to continue to develop league tables for identifying poor performers, it will be extremely important for indicators such as CFR to determine the most appropriate ways of calculating them. As can be seen from this preliminary study, varying the time intervals from admission to death, location of death and different ways of recording cause of death can have a major effect on whether CFRs adjusted for age group and sex for individual hospitals differ significantly from a reference hospital.

Early results from further work in progress show that other factors such as including deaths in hospital not recorded on PAS and sudden deaths outside hospital in mortality rate calculations may also have a major effect on league table positions.

Until the most robust and clinically appropriate methods of calculating AMI mortality rates have been determined, these population and hospital outcome indicators should be used with great care.

References

1   Birkhead J, Goldacre M, Mason A, Wilkinson E, *et al* (eds). *Health outcome indicators: myocardial infarction.* Report of a working group to the Department of Health. Oxford: National Centre for Health Outcomes Development, 1999.

2   Department of Health. *National service framework for coronary heart disease: modern standards and service models.* London: DoH, 2000.

3   Birkhead JS, Norris R, Quinn T, Pearson M. *Acute myocardial infarction: a core data set for monitoring standards of care.* London: Royal College of Physicians, 1999.

4 | Hospital league tables and how to avoid relegation

Iain Findlay

Reactions to the hospital outcome data

This chapter presents a personal view, as a consultant cardiologist responsible for service delivery, of my response to the hospital outcome indicators (HOI). The first outcome indicators were constructed for Scottish hospitals during the early 1990s. The initial intention was to publish them as anonymised data. My first view of the indicators for acute myocardial infarction (AMI) provoked in me a mixed reaction and range of emotions, largely due to initial misinterpretations of the data. When I saw my hospital placing (this may reflect the personality of a cardiologist) I naturally assumed that we were amongst the best hospitals with one of the lowest 30-day mortality. Unfortunately, the table referred to survival rates (Fig 1).

My shock on reading this table – that was indeed my reaction – was tempered by the fact that the intention was to publish the data in an *anonymised* fashion. However, this intention did not last, and it was decided that the clinical HOIs were to be 'named' data[1]. I had taken over the running of coronary care from my general medical colleagues, and did not readily relish the prospect of appearing in the press as being responsible for the second or third worst performing hospital in Scotland. As the sole cardiologist, it was clear who was going to take any blame if this was to be apportioned.

Wider concerns then began to arise in my mind. I worried about the reaction of future patients:

▪ How many coming into our coronary care unit (CCU) would be aware of our poor record?

▪ How many relatives of deceased patients would be left wondering if things 'might have been different' if their relative had been treated in one of the nearby Glasgow teaching hospitals?

After more reflection, what was left of the clinical investigator in me surfaced and I felt that I had to do something more constructive. This involved examining the data in greater detail.

Were our survival data bad?

I recognised that it was imperative to examine directly the suggestion that our survival figures were 'bad'. In order to get something positive from this

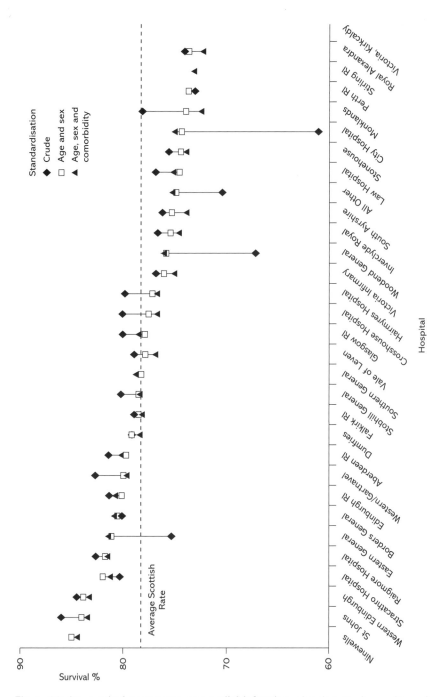

Fig 1. 30-day survival post-acute myocardial infarction, showing crude results and standardised for age and sex, and for age, sex and comorbidity (RI = Royal Infirmary).

episode, I used it as an impetus to evaluate our treatment of AMI to see if and where improvements could be made. This investigation subsequently led to a more general consideration of whether the HOIs were sufficiently able to take confounding variables and other factors into account.

I was given a great deal of assistance and encouragement in undertaking this examination from the Information and Statistics Division (ISD) of the Common Services Agency in Scotland, from Dr Steve Kendrick in particular.

Accuracy of data

ISD were confident that their data were statistically accurate. Scotland has a well developed and comprehensively validated record linkage system. It was unlikely that this system would be the source of inaccuracy to explain our poor performance[2]. I was however disturbed by the rather unquestioning acceptance of the accuracy of what was called 'clinical data'. 'Rubbish in rubbish out' sprang to mind. Discussions with Dr Kendrick rapidly revealed what I believed was a disturbing lack of clinical input into the creation and interpretation of the ISD data set.

Mortality data

It became apparent that mortality from AMI varied, and thus the ranking of hospitals, if it was measured using data generated from only the first diagnostic coding field, or the first and second fields of the coding return. Thus, the clinical outcome indicators could differ if a death from AMI was returned as:

1 Acute myocardial infarction.
2 Left ventricular failure.

– rather than:

1 Left ventricular failure.
2 Acute myocardial infarction.

Coding decisions

Another disturbing feature was that the ISD outcome indicators, as published in a peer-review journal[3], clearly purported to relate to *all* admissions to hospital with AMI. As the article stated:

> *The outcome indicator adopted was 30-day mortality after* admission to hospital
> with a principal diagnosis of acute myocardial infarction *(ICD9 code 410)*

– my italics. The codes used by ISD in fact refer to *discharge* diagnosis and not *admission* diagnosis. Despite the problems inherent in this, the practice persists. There are many possible instances where the conflation of these two outcomes can affect performance. For example, there is convincing evidence in the literature that the most common perceived cause of death in a community is entered into a death certificate in cases of sudden unexpected or uncertain death. Thus, a hospital with an on-site geriatric long-stay unit could have its rate of death from AMI artificially inflated if all sudden deaths of uncertain or unexplained cause are recorded as death from AMI. In large hospitals with acute surgical units many deaths from surgery are not consequential on the operation *per se* but due to peri-operative infarction.

Even more fundamentally, who determines or could predict how death is recorded in someone who dies from AMI following acute admission with fracture neck of femur? Is it (1) fracture neck of femur, (2) AMI – or vice versa? It appears that coding departments may play as critical a role as doctors in determining performance.

The potential for error to arise from coding decisions was evident in our department. In 1992, I reviewed the records of patients admitted to our CCU with AMI and drew some comparisons with the Scottish Morbidity Record (SMR) coding discharge data. Our CCU admissions records book listed 47 deaths in coronary care, but the SMR 1 data indicated only 35 deaths. Furthermore, according to the CCU admissions book, 264 patients with AMI were discharged to the medical wards, but the SMR data showed only 229 such patients were transferred. Of the patients with a CCU diagnosis of AMI who were discharged alive to the general medical wards, 35 were not given a final SMR coded diagnosis at discharge of having had an AMI. In short, these two data records purport to measure the same outcomes but convey different pictures.

Audit of deaths

In two separate two-month time periods I then audited 17 deaths in our hospital which had been returned to ISD coded as deaths from AMI. (The discharge diagnosis is entered in a coding form completed by medical staff; this is then transcribed by hospital coding staff.) Only 11 of the 17 had a cardiovascular discharge diagnosis (AMI (9); ischaemic heart disease (IHD) (2)) entered by medical staff on the coding form. Five further patients had, respectively, a diagnosis of pulmonary embolism, respiratory failure, liver failure, hyperkalaemic cardiac arrest secondary to chronic renal failure and hypothermia. The remaining patient was dead on arrival in accident and emergency (A&E). An examination of the case records of the 11 with codes of AMI or IHD as cause of death revealed that the diagnosis provided by medical staff was incorrect in four patients. Three of them had died, respectively, of stroke, left ventricular failure and renal failure. The cause of death of the fourth was unknown.

Non-clinical influences on published indicators

Given the clinical and political importance of HOIs, I will labour the point regarding the effect and possible implications of non-clinical factors continuing to influence the indicators to be published in the future. The Scottish data showed clearly that the 30-day survival of recognised AMI is related to the proportion of recognised cases of AMI admitted to hospital (Fig 2). One variable thought to influence hospital mortality rates is the speed of admission to hospital. Conventional wisdom suggested that larger infarcts would cause more pain and result in a quicker call for help. The argument ran that those individuals with bigger infarcts were more likely to be admitted to hospital, and that faster ambulance response times would further worsen mortality figures. In fact, the opposite was the case. The data indicate that a simple way to improve a hospital performance without doing anything clinically different is to increase the number of AMIs admitted to hospital.

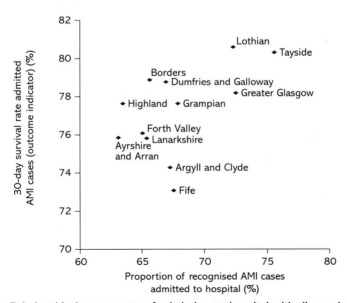

Fig 2. Relationship between rate of admission to hospital with diagnosis of acute myocardial infarction (AMI) and 30-day mortality by health board in Scotland (1989–1991).

Investigation of underperforming areas

In addition to these general concerns with coding and information recording, I remained distressed by the unfavourable survival that we were recorded as having. I endeavoured to undertake a rigorous examination to determine any areas in which we were not performing effectively.

My more general concerns with data coding were not assuaged by further interpretation of the ISD data. The initial data from ISD generated some significant inconsistencies that led to further questions regarding the validity of the data. For example, the data showed an inverse relationship between the 30-day mortality from AMI and the number of AMI per 1,000 of the population: that is, mortality rates were lower in those areas with the highest rates of diagnosed AMI. It was puzzling that areas acknowledged to have high rates of coronary heart disease (CHD) (eg Fife) could be shown to have a *lower* rate of AMI per 1,000 population admitted to hospital than health boards in relatively affluent areas (eg Tayside) with a lower rate of heart disease. This is most easily explained by the criteria used to diagnose AMI.

Cardiac enzymes and diagnosis

We surveyed all the CCUs in Scotland at that time and found that a variety of cardiac enzymes were used to diagnose AMI (Table 1). It could well be that increased rates of AMI reflect the inclusion of smaller infarcts diagnosed by creatine kinase (CK) or CKMB. This would have a beneficial effect on mortality by raising the denominator (number of AMI) without affecting the numerator (deaths from MI), as those with smaller infarcts have a better prognosis. The effect on diagnostic sensitivity can be judged from data derived from 50 patients admitted to our unit with AMI (Table 2).

Standardised mortality ratio

A major inconsistency, to my mind, in the accuracy of statistics pertaining to CHD was that the standardised mortality ratio for the population served by our hospital was higher than the Scottish average but we had a lower than average hospital discharge rate. These data were provided by a needs care assessment (NCA) carried out by our health authority (Argyll and Clyde Health Board). These were also the data returned to ISD. The NCA covering the period of the HOIs showed that the recorded rate of admission with AMI for established cases (patients with a previous

Table 1. Enzymes used to diagnose acute myocardial infarction in 24 Scottish coronary care units in 1995.

Enzyme	Routine		Request	
	No.	%	No.	%
Aspartate aminotransferase	16	67	–	–
Lactate dehydrogenase	12	50	–	–
Creatine kinase	20	83	1	4
Creatine kinase-MB	2	8	12	50
Hydroxybutyric dehydrogenase	1	4	–	–

Source: Telephone survey, 1995.

Table 2. Sensitivity of cardiac enzymes in 50 patients with acute myocardial infarction (40 Q wave, 10 non-Q wave).

Enzyme	Admission	% positive			Sensitivity (%)
		6 hours	12 hours	24 hours	
Aspartate aminotransferase	12	66	77	74	84
Lactate dehydrogenase	6	32	43	58	68
Creatine kinase	27	88	94	76	98
Myoglobin	51	92	76	48	98
Troponin quantitative	36	98	100	100	100
Troponin stick test*	24	92	98	98	98

*A method of new patient testing.

admission diagnosis of CHD) was lower than the Scottish average (141 vs 191 per 100,000 and 68 vs 95 per 100,000 for men and women, respectively).

This suggested to me that there had been either an under-referral of patients with AMI to hospital during the period studied or a significant failure to record their admission. Local general practitioners confirmed that they still treated a significant number of AMI patients at home at that time. If so, this was likely to be those who were least ill. If cases with previous AMI/CHD were not recorded and returned to ISD, this would have a significant effect on the recorded incidence of cardiac comorbidity on the population admitted to our hospital with AMI in the period studied for the HOIs. Cardiac comorbidity of any kind resulted in a doubling of the 30-day mortality in the analysis reported by Capewell et al[3]. Thus, some of our apparent excess mortality may well be due to previous under-recording of admission with AMI/CHD. Interestingly, mortality from AMI for patients with established CHD was *lower* than the Scottish average, strikingly so in women. There is no logical reason why we should be good at treating established cases but not incident cases (cases with no previous history of admission with CHD in the past five years), particularly as the former can be expected to be more problematic.

UK audit of patients admitted to hospital with chest pain

I also considered what was the true incidence of established CHD in patients admitted to the hospital. At that time, we were participating in the UK audit of patients admitted to CCU with chest pain run by Dr John Birkhead[4]. This showed that patients admitted to our CCU with chest pain had the second highest incidence of previous angina recorded (52%) and the fifth highest percentage of previous AMI (37%) among the 22 hospitals in the audit. This was at variance with the 'official' rate in Argyle and Clyde Health Board's NCA.

Diagnosis

In terms of admission diagnosis, we were comparable with the other units:

▪ firm admission diagnosis of AMI: 21% of our patients

▪ possible AMI: 11%

▪ unstable angina: 27%

▪ final diagnosis of AMI: 32% (lower than the group average of 39%).

Performance

There were many encouraging signs from the study about our performance. In terms of getting patients into coronary care (ie from time of onset of symptoms to arrival in CCU), we were the quickest unit in the study. In comparison with the other units, the same percentage (71%) of patients with AMI received thrombolytic therapy. Where the diagnosis of AMI was certain, our door-to-needle time was slightly better than the group average (51 min vs a group mean of 62 min). Where the diagnosis was uncertain, our mean delay before making a decision was 155 minutes versus 130 minutes for the group.

This is not to imply that we were entirely happy with our performance (see below). We believed, for instance, that the time spent in A&E could be improved from the 42-minute average. However, nothing in these data suggested that our CCU was not as efficient and rigorous in responding to admissions and administering thrombolytic therapy as other hospitals.

Coronary care unit mortality from acute myocardial infarction

I was also fortunate in obtaining clinical trial data, kindly provided by the investigators of the many thrombolytic trials in which we had previously participated. This enabled us to compare our mortality in CCU for AMI with the trial average. These figures suggested that we did not compare adversely with other sites in terms of mortality or treatment given. For example, 90% of our patients entered into the International Study of Infarct Survival (ISIS)-4[5] received streptokinase compared with 77% of patients across the sites studied.

Admissions to hospital

Examination of admissions to our hospital covering the same period as the HOIs showed that the number of patients discharged with a diagnosis of AMI remained constant at around 530 per annum. I broke the data down into patients admitted to the CCU and compared them with other hospital wards which included geriatrics (Table 3). Patients admitted outwith CCU were significantly older and had a significantly higher death rate, particularly women.

The admissions for AMI in 1992 to the general medical unit and CCU were examined in greater detail:

▮ overall in-hospital mortality: 20%
▮ mortality in patients not admitted to CCU: 27%
▮ mortality in patients admitted to CCU: 15%.

It was noteworthy that even during this one year we could show a significant difference between those receiving thrombolytic therapy (streptokinase) and those who did not:

▮ overall CCU mortality: 15%
▮ mortality in patients receiving streptokinase: 12%
▮ mortality in those not receiving streptokinase: 18%.

Validity of hospital outcome data

Overall, I continue to be dissatisfied with the validity of the HOIs in terms of what these data convey about the quality of care that patients actually receive. Even a cursory examination of the indicators suggests that many factors related to coding and clinical definitions potentially impinge on a

Table 3. Mortality in patients admitted/not admitted to the coronary care unit with a final diagnosis of acute myocardial infarction.

	Male			Female		
Year	No.	Mean age	In-hospital mortality (%)	No.	Mean age	In-hospital mortality (%)
Coronary care unit						
1991	87	62	23	37	69	16
1992	166	63	22	74	65	20
1993	172	62	10	94	67	22
To Sept 1994	131	65	8	81	70	19
Not coronary care unit						
1991	163	69	19	113	77	33
1992	140	71	26	154	79	38
1993	115	72	38	137	77	44
To Sept 1994	86	68	27	107	75	29

unit's recorded (as opposed to actual) performance. I hope for the future that clinicians will play a greater role in formulating and discussing the nature, uses and misuses of the HOIs. As regards the cardiology services for which I am responsible, although the HOIs conveyed a potentially erroneous account of the quality of care, I believe they contributed to the further strengthening of our services.

Recommendations

Following publication of the HOIs, I was asked to make recommendations. I submitted the following suggestions, all of which have been implemented in our hospital:

1 All patients with AMI should be admitted to the CCU.
2 The number of beds in CCU be increased from four to six.
3 CCU be integrated into the medical unit to create a mini-cardiology department to ensure greater medical input, particularly consultant input, into the care of patients with AMI.
4 Give thrombolysis in A&E to reduce door-to-needle time.
5 Develop a prescribing policy in CCU to increase use of aspirin, beta-blockers and angiotensin-converting enzyme inhibitors.
6 Ideally, patients who have a complicated course in hospital and all patients with non-Q wave AMI should be followed up by a cardiologist.

7 Give consideration to a post-AMI clinic to ensure optimum uptake of secondary prevention.

8 Consider setting up a formal resuscitation committee in lieu of the establishment of a resuscitation officer, and train all senior nurses in the medical unit in defibrillation.

9 The establishment of a CCU computer database in order to spot trends and institute any necessary changes quickly.

Conclusion

The HOIs affected me personally and had an effect on my professional confidence. I was supported by my colleagues and by hospital management who encouraged me to find an explanation for our supposed poor performance. My fears of professional crucifixion were not justified. In fact, if anything, the opposite was the case. I was surprised at the relatively brief attention paid to the HOIs – so much so that I still question their value.

It may be that things will be different in England. I hope that what transpired in Scotland transpires in England. In Scotland, it was appreciated from the beginning by influential public health doctors that this is not the way to compare hospital performance. Rather than use crude mortality rates it is better to assess performance by looking at clinical practice, particularly the use of proven treatments (eg thrombolysis, door-to-needle times, aspirin, etc).

The Clinical Standards Board

In Scotland, the Clinical Standards Board (CSB) has come into existence (see http://www.clinicalstandards.org/; the actual standards for AMI can be found at: http://www.clinicalstandards.org/standards.asp). The CSB has statutory powers and has set standards for the care of AMI. Every hospital in Scotland has been assessed and visited by volunteer health professionals and lay members of the public. A report will be published for each hospital with the aim of promoting confidence in our hospital service.

I have been both an assessor and an assessed and have every confidence that this is the way forward. Similar standards have been set by the national service framework for CHD[6]. It can only be hoped that these will render HOIs redundant.

Remaining concerns

It still concerns me that such important information that affects public confidence can be published without major clinical input. It does not take a genius to look at the HOIs to appreciate that the differences in survival between different hospitals were so great that they could not be the result of hospital treatment. Some of the differences were so large that the differing mortality could not be accounted for even if one hospital gave no treatment and another all known treatments.

PS: Figures for 1999 showed our hospital to have an above average 30-day survival (I have double-checked this!).

References

1   Clinical Resource and Audit Group (CRAG). *The third report from the Clinical Outcomes Working Group. Clinical outcome indicators.* Edinburgh: Scottish Home and Health Department, 1994:2.17–2.19.

2   Kendrick S, Clarke J. The Scottish Record Linkage System. *Health Bull (Edinb)* 1993;**51**:72–9.

3   Capewell S, Kendrick S, Boyd J. Cohen G, *et al.* Measuring outcomes: one month survival after acute myocardial infarction in Scotland. *Heart* 1996;**76**:70–5.

4   Birkhead JS. Thrombolytic treatment for myocardial infarction: an examination of practice in 39 United Kingdom hospitals. Myocardial Infarction Audit Group. *Heart* 1997;**78**:28–33.

5   ISIS-4: a randomised factorial trial assessing early oral captopril, oral mononitrate, and intravenous magnesium sulphate in 58,050 patients with suspected acute myocardial infarction. ISIS-4 (Fourth International Study of Infarct Survival) Collaborative Group. *Lancet* 1995;**345**:669–85.

6   Department of Health. *National service framework for coronary heart disease: modern standards and service models.* London: DoH, 2000.

5 | Should we use process or outcome measures to assess quality of care?

Jonathan Mant

There is a role for both outcome measures such as mortality and process measures such as uptake of fibrinolysis in assessing quality of care in acute myocardial infarction (AMI). In making decisions about which to use, the following are important considerations:

1 Breadth of perspective required.

2 Strengths and weaknesses of outcome and process measures.

3 For what reason are the data being collected?

Breadth of perspective required

Since McKeown's landmark analysis[1] of the reasons for the improvements in human health over the course of the nineteenth and first half of the twentieth century, we have been aware that medical care is only one of several factors that can be responsible for changes in population health. If healthcare is monitored using mortality rates, it forces us to consider those influences outside the healthcare system that might have had an effect. For example, coronary heart disease (CHD) age-specific mortality over the course of the twentieth century increased until the mid-1970s in both males and females, and has been falling since then (shown for males in Fig 1)[2]. Thus, in 45–54 year old males, mortality from ischaemic heart disease went up from 0.4 per 1,000 in 1921 to 2.7 per 1,000 in 1971. It is not clear what caused the twentieth century epidemic of CHD, but some circumstantial evidence suggests that changes in lifestyle, notably diet and smoking, have played a major role in both the rise and fall of the disease[2].

In Scotland, there was a 29% reduction in age-adjusted mortality for CHD between 1975 and 1994[3]. It has been estimated that 60% of this decline can be accounted for by changes in population risk factors, and 40% by changes in treatment of AMI, secondary prevention, angina, heart failure and hypertension (Fig 2)[3]. The largest single factor was the decline in smoking prevalence (46% to 28% in men, 37% to 25% in women); this was estimated to account for 36% of the total decline in CHD mortality. An analysis of the 24% decline in CHD mortality rates in Auckland, New Zealand, between 1982 and 1993 reached similar conclusions as to the

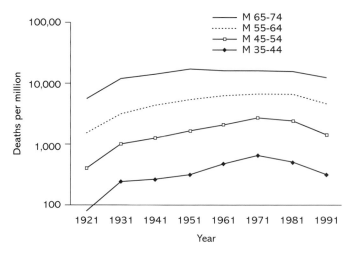

Fig 1. **Age-specific mortality in England and Wales from ischaemic heart disease 1921-1991 (men aged 35–74 years)**[2].

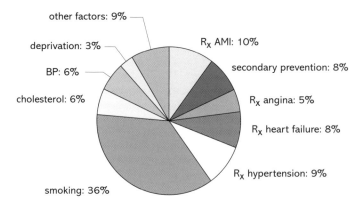

Fig 2. **Reasons for reduced coronary heart disease mortality, Scotland 1975–1994**[3] (BP = blood pressure; AMI = myocardial infarction; R_x = treatment).

relative importance of decline in smoking prevalence as an explanation of the downward trend[4].

A narrower perspective is obtained by consideration of mortality following admission to hospital with AMI. Data from the Oxford Myocardial Infarction Incidence Study show that 70% of all the deaths within 28 days of AMI in the study (519) occurred in people who never reached hospital, the majority of whom received no medical attention prior to death (Fig 3)[5].

Thus, focusing on hospital-specific mortality moves the agenda from prevention (the most practical strategy for reducing overall mortality

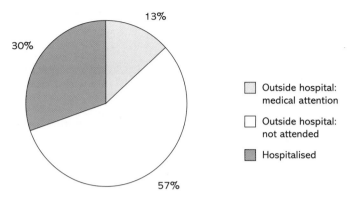

13%

30%

57%

☐ Outside hospital:
   medical attention

☐ Outside hospital:
   not attended

▨ Hospitalised

Fig 3. 28-day mortality from myocardial infarction[5].

from AMI) to treatment. Focusing on process narrows the perspective still further; this concentrates attention entirely on specific aspects of medical care, and implicitly excludes consideration of the broader determinants of outcome following AMI. As discussed below, whether or not this is appropriate depends upon the purpose for which the monitoring is performed.

Strengths and weaknesses of outcome and process measures

The ability to detect differences in quality of care

The advantages and disadvantages of outcome measures compared with process measures are summarised in Table 1. An important consideration is the extent to which the different measures are able to detect differences in quality of care between hospitals, or indeed between the same hospital over time. An intrinsic advantage of process measures is that they are more sensitive than outcome measures to differences in the quality of care.

Table 1. Outcome versus process monitoring.

Outcome	Process
Insensitive to differences in quality of care	Sensitive to differences in quality of care
Difficult to interpret	Easy to interpret
Relevant if no evidence	Inappropriate if no evidence
Can reflect many aspects of process of care	Can measure only a few aspects of care
Useful where technical expertise important	Cannot measure technical expertise
Intuitively important	Worthy but dull

This can be illustrated by considering the quality of treatment for AMI between hospitals. It has been estimated that optimal use of proven interventions in the treatment of AMI (eg fibrinolysis, aspirin, beta-blockade, angiotensin converting enzyme inhibitors) could potentially reduce mortality for AMI by up to 45%[6].

Table 2 shows how many patients would need to be monitored to detect significant differences in the uptake of proven interventions, and how long it would take to detect significant differences in outcome attributable to the difference in uptake if we want to compare performance in two hospitals. At one extreme, if one hospital uses effective interventions 6% of the time, the difference in process of care compared with another hospital that does not use these interventions would be detectable at a significance level of 5% and 80% power if the care of 155 patients was monitored in each hospital. This would be expected to lead to a reduction in mortality from 30% to 29%, which translates to 4.5 lives saved per year in a typical hospital with 450 admissions annually for AMI. To detect this mortality difference at the same significance level and power would require monitoring 32,846 patients – the equivalent of a 73-year study! Larger differences in the process of care would be expected to lead to mortality differences detectable over feasible lengths of time. Thus, a difference in uptake from 0% to 31% would be expected to lead to a 5% reduction in mortality (from 30% to 25%) which would be detected in a three-year study, and a change from 0% to 55% would be detected in a one-year study.

This analysis is likely to have overestimated the sensitivity of outcome measurement, in that it is based on generous assumptions about both the additive effect of different interventions on outcome and high baseline mortality for AMI cases admitted to hospital.

Table 2. Sensitivity of process and outcome measures to differences in quality of care[6].

Difference in:		No. of lives saved per year	No. of patients needed to detect difference†	
Mortality	Uptake of proven drugs*		Mortality	Use of drugs
30% vs 29%	0% vs 6%	4.5	32,846	155
30% vs 25%	0% vs 31%	22.5	1,290	27
30% vs 21%	0% vs 55%	40.5	389	12

* thrombolysis, aspirin, beta-blockers, angiotensin-converting enzyme inhibitors.
† $p < 0.05$, 80% power.

The interpretation of observed differences

A second consideration is the problem of interpretation of observed differences.

In the previous example, it was assumed that any observed statistically significant differences in outcome would be due to differences in quality of care – since in every other respect the hospitals and the patients were assumed to be identical. In reality, if differences in outcome are observed, other explanations need to be considered (Fig 4). The observed differences may simply be due to not comparing like with like, either because of differences in case-mix, including factors such as comorbidity and severity of infarct, or because of differences in how cases were found and defined.

Conversely, differences in process of care are easier to interpret: the more people without contraindications who receive fibrinolysis after AMI the better. The problems of not comparing like with like can be minimised in several ways, by:

■ undertaking prospective data collection
■ developing more sophisticated case-mix adjustment systems
■ standardising methods of case ascertainment and case definition, and
■ training staff so that data are recorded and collected in a consistent way.

Standardisation also needs to apply to the case-mix data. In the USA, there were dramatic increases in the apparent prevalence of risk factors for poor outcome from cardiac surgery following the introduction of a case-mix adjusted outcome monitoring system. For example, the proportion of patients with chronic obstructive pulmonary disease increased from 7% to 17% associated with a fall in case-mix adjusted mortality[7]. Does this reflect better quality of care or simply a change in how risk factors are recorded?

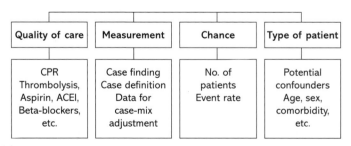

Quality of care	Measurement	Chance	Type of patient
CPR Thrombolysis, Aspirin, ACEI, Beta-blockers, etc.	Case finding Case definition Data for case-mix adjustment	No. of patients Event rate	Potential confounders Age, sex, comorbidity, etc.

Fig 4. Explanations for variations in outcome (ACEI = angiotensin-converting enzyme inhibitor; CPR = cardiopulmonary resuscitation).

Other considerations

On the other hand, process measures are inappropriate if there is no evidence for a given intervention or procedure. They are not good at capturing other aspects of quality of care which might influence mortality, such as the skill of the cardiac arrest team or the ability of the medical staff to identify and treat complications as they develop. Furthermore, mortality will reflect the sum of all aspects of care, whereas process measures will tend to concentrate on a few. An important consideration is that process measures can record *whether* something is done, but not *how* it is done. This probably does not matter for the administration of drugs, but is likely to be important where interventions require technical expertise such as surgery[8]. Finally, outcome measurement, unlike process measurement, is concerned with what would intuitively be regarded as important.

For what reason are the data being collected?

The relative importance of these different strengths and weaknesses of outcome and process measures depends upon the purpose for which the data are being collected. If the aim is to inform health policy and strategy, mortality data are much more useful than process data. Such data generate consideration of influences on health outside the healthcare sector, while within healthcare they focus attention on prevention as well as treatment.

If, however, the aim is to improve quality of hospital care through clinical audit, process measures are much more useful than outcome measures in the case of AMI. They are more sensitive, easier to interpret, and the necessary action to complete the audit cycle is likely to be clear. While case-mix adjustment systems can be developed to make differences in outcome easier to interpret, the expense of standardising and ensuring quality control of data collection is likely to outweigh any benefits outside specific research projects.

Both process and outcome measures have a role in service agreements:

▪ *process measures* to provide an external stimulus to hospitals to provide evidence-based care, and

▪ *outcome measures* to allow the commissioner, whether primary care group or health authority, to put the performance into the context of the health targets for CHD[9].

Identifying poor performers

In the light of the controversy surrounding paediatric heart surgery in Bristol[10], it is tempting to use mortality variations as a means to identify poor performers, but it is unlikely to have much of a role in identifying poor performers in the treatment of AMI. Apart from the potential adverse consequences of looking for 'bad apples'[11], it is unlikely that routine data will be of sufficient quality to allow robust conclusions to be drawn without significant expense. Indeed, it has been argued that routine analysis of mortality data might not have been able to identify the murders committed by Shipman[12]. Risk management techniques that focus on the analysis and investigation of individual incidents rather than seeking to interpret statistical variations offer a more efficient, and probably more effective, mechanism for both identifying and addressing such problems.

Outcome data

Outcome data are unlikely to improve consumer choice about where to be treated for AMI. People have only limited choice as to where they are treated, and the data are difficult to interpret. Nevertheless, public availability of the data could contribute to informed debate over local healthcare provision and raise public awareness of the key issues.

Conclusion

There is a role for monitoring both process and outcome of AMI. However, to improve the quality of care, the emphasis should be on well-conducted audits of the process of care rather than on potentially costly case-mix adjustment of outcome. This conclusion does not necessarily apply to other areas of healthcare. It will depend principally, first, on the extent to which there is an evidence base for treatment and, secondly, on how much the quality of care, in particular technical care, is likely to influence outcome.

References

1   McKeown T. *The role of medicine: drama, mirage, miracle or nemesis,* 2nd edn. Oxford: Blackwell, 1979.
2   Charlton J, Murphy M, Khaw K, Ebrahim S, Smith GD. Cardiovascular diseases. In: Charlton J, Murphy M (eds). *The health of adult Britain, 1841-1991,* vol 2. London: The Stationery Office 1997:60–81.
3   Capewell S, Morrison CE, McMurray JJ. Contribution of modern cardiovascular treatment and risk factor changes to the decline in coronary heart disease mortality in Scotland between 1975 and 1994. *Heart* 1999;**81**:380–6.
4   Capewell S, Beaglehole R, Seddon M, McMurray J. Explanation for the decline in coronary heart disease mortality rates in Auckland, New Zealand, between 1982 and 1993. *Circulation* 2000;**102**:1511–6.
5   Volmink JA, Newton JN, Hicks NR, Sleight P, *et al.* Coronary event and case fatality rates in an English population: results of the Oxford Myocardial Infarction Incidence Study. *Heart* 1998;**80**:40–4.

6   Mant J, Hicks N. Detecting differences in quality of care: the sensitivity of measures of process and outcome in treating acute myocardial infarction. *Br Med J* 1995;**311**:793–6.

7   Green J, Wintfield N. Report cards on cardiac surgeons. Assessing New York State's approach. *N Engl J Med* 1995;**332**:1229–32.

8   Mant J, Hicks NR. Assessing quality of care: what are the implications of the potential lack of sensitivity of outcome measures to differences in quality? *J Eval Clin Pract* 1996;**2**:243–8.

9   Secretary of State for Health. *Saving lives: our healthier nation.* Cm 4386. London: The Stationery Office, 1999.

10 Smith R. All changed, changed utterly. British medicine will be transformed by the Bristol case. *Br Med J* 1998;**316**:1917–8.

11 Berwick DM. Continuous improvement as an ideal in health care. *N Engl J Med* 1989;**320**:53–6.

12 Frankel S, Sterne J, Smith GD. Mortality variations as a measure of general practitioner performance: implications of the Shipman case. *Br Med J* 2000;**320**:489.

6 | Implementing the national service framework for coronary heart disease

Rod Griffiths

Implementing a programme for change

Implementing a programme such as a national service framework (NSF) for coronary heart disease[1] requires management of change across a large complex system – and few systems are as large or as complex as the NHS. In a management sense, by 'complex' I mean different layers of interests driven by different imperatives, histories and cultures. What drives a specialist registrar will be different to some extent from what drives a ward sister, a consultant or a general practitioner (GP), but they may all have some clinical issues in common. A support service manager will respond to a quite different set of motivators, and comes with a different history and understanding. Chief executives and other board members will be different again. If change is to be managed effectively, all these interests – or at least enough of them – have to be identified and brought into line.

The second issue to clarify is whether we are trying to change people or systems. In 'systems', I include both the procedures and protocols that are supposed to describe intended actions and the hardware that we use. Getting a new machine for a particular task or introducing a new test in the management of patients is different from getting people to use the kit or take the right action when the test has been done. The people aspects are usually the hardest so I will concentrate on them.

I find the work of Beckard among the most useful in this regard[2]. He produces flow charts and tables that assist thinking about both diagnosing the problem and implementing change. The simplest of these charts categorises all possible players in a change as to whether they are likely to:

▪ get in the way

▪ be passive

▪ help, or

▪ really work to make it happen.

This may sound manipulative, but once that classification is clear in our mind we can start to think what it would take to change those who are in the way and to encourage the helpers. We may decide that some of the blockers are unimportant and can be ignored. Another chart helps to clarify the importance of different actors.

Ethical approach

If we take it upon ourselves to behave in this sort of way, trying to understand people's motives and manipulate either them or the situation in order to achieve change, it is important to behave in an ethical manner. Medical ethics exist, among other things, to protect patients from those who could use their position and knowledge to exploit them. I believe the same is true of change management techniques. For instance, assassination has a strong evidence base as a change management tool and is apparently still used in some parts of the world, but we reject it on ethical grounds.

How to encourage change

There is of course considerable theory in the psychological literature about how people change, and it is worthy of study[3]. Giving up smoking and beginning to wash your hands as often as you should probably have much in common. It is also clear that a lot must be left to the individual. The Secretary of State sitting in Whitehall cannot tell an individual doctor or nurse what to do with a particular patient. He has to trust the person on the ground.

There are a few actions that can be taken to help to ensure the right outcome is more likely. Although, in the end, we have to trust the person on the job, we can for instance:

▪ ensure that staff who are appointed are up to the job
▪ train and retrain
▪ provide the right equipment and enough staff.

Teamwork

Another common mistake is to concentrate too much on the abilities of the apparently key players. It is all very well to have George Best on your team but if no one gives him the ball the team still does not do very well. Furthermore, some of these prima donnas can be rather difficult to manage and may actually disrupt a reasonable team. How often have we seen a football team with fantastically expensive stars still go down the league? The same can happen with any team, including a medical one: it is the team that counts, not just the individual players. Again, the psychology and management literature is full of material to understand how teams work and how to build better ones. It is remarkable how little it seems to be read.

The West Midlands Thrombolysis Project

In the mid-1990s a number of audits of thrombolysis times were carried out in hospitals across the West Midlands. It was clear from these audits that although most patients who should have had thrombolysis received it, they rarely got it quickly – yet the evidence, as everyone now knows, is that time matters.

The directors of public health were persuaded that a region-wide project to reduce pain-to-needle time made sense. For this to happen, everyone involved had to be lined up. The key players were believed to be:

- chief executives of health authorities and trusts
- cardiologists, general physicians and accident and emergency consultants
- chairmen and non-executives of health authorities and trusts
- ambulance trusts and their staff, and
- various nursing groups.

Initial planning

A meeting was held with each group at which they were presented with the evidence that pain-to-needle time should be reduced. Any problems envisaged by the group were addressed. When the round of consultation was complete the regional health authority was asked to approve a project which involved all the acute trusts in the region joining the British Cardiac Society/Royal College of Physicians national thrombolysis audit[4].

The aim of the project

The essence of the project was to measure the component parts of the pain-to-needle time and feed the data back to the clinicians and managers in individual hospitals so that they could see how they were doing. The change management manipulation was of course to have set things up so that it mattered to each of the key participants that they were not the worst. Simply making people uncomfortable by feeding their data back is not enough. Two other factors were found to be important:

1 To have a co-ordinator who could ensure the quality of the data across the system and disseminate good practice in a non-threatening way.

2 The adoption of external standards, so that there was a valid benchmark at which to aim, irrespective of the performance of others. In effect, hospitals were competing with themselves to achieve the standard.

The importance of standards

Standards are interesting: the word derives from the flags that ancient armies carried to battle. In warfare, they serve many purposes: they are a rallying point visible above the heat of the battle, and they represent the unit to which they are attached. They are owned and valued. The same has to be true of standards in NSFs. They must be:

▪ visible to all

▪ owned by all

▪ arrived at by consensus, and

▪ valued and respected.

If these conditions are fulfilled, standards represent something we can rally round and they are a potent engine for change.

Results of the project

Using these principles, the West Midlands Thrombolysis Project achieved a significant amount of change over its first three years.

The first finding was that if a patient is seen at home by the GP this can result in delay unless the GP gives thrombolysis immediately (Fig 1).

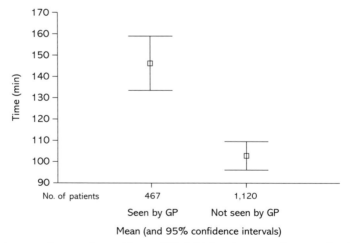

Fig 1. Impact of general practitioner (GP) initial action on call-to-needle time for patients eligible for thrombolysis, West Midlands Thrombolysis Project, year 3.

Having seen this result, the data were fed back to the GPs, reminding them that the best response to a call that sounded like an obvious infarct was to dial 999. The ensuing change in behaviour by the GPs increased the proportion of patients going direct to hospital and reduced delay.

Figures 2 and 3 show the reduction in door-to-needle and call-to-door times achieved across the region as a whole during the period of the project. These changes have been maintained and increased in subsequent years. Our last quarter's data showed that the median door-to-needle

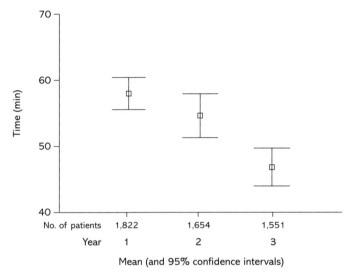

Fig 2. Time trend in door-to-needle time for patients eligible for thrombolysis, West Midlands Thrombolysis Project, years 1–3.

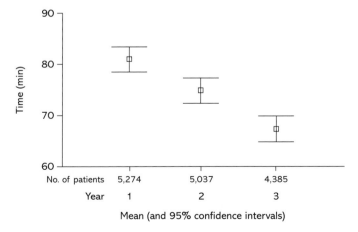

Fig 3. Time trend in call-to-door time (all patients with suspected acute myocardial infarction), West Midlands Thrombolysis Project, years 1–3.

time is now 30 minutes, with 52% of cases across the region treated in 30 minutes or less.

These changes began to take place only once a comprehensive project was in place. Nothing like this occurred following previous individual audits, and at the time of the project the national study was not showing similar changes. This reduction in delay should have resulted in a considerable saving of life. The results of the project demonstrate that an organised approach to change management, combined with audit data, can achieve much more than audit or exhortation alone.

References

1   Department of Health. *National service framework for coronary heart disease: modern standards and service models.* London: DoH, 2000.

2   Beckard R, Harris RT. Organizational transitions: managing complex change. Wokingham: Addison-Wesley, 1987.

3   Iles V, Sutherland K. *Managing change in the NHS: organisational change – a review for health care managers, professionals and researchers.* London: National Co-ordinating Centre for NHS Service Delivery and Organisation Research & Development, 2001.

4   Birkhead JS. Thrombolytic treatment for myocardial infarction: an examination of practice in 39 United Kingdom hospitals. Myocardial Infarction Audit Group. *Heart* 1997;**78**:28–33.

7 | National benchmarking in asthma and stroke: role of the Clinical Effectiveness and Evaluation Unit in national audit

Mike Pearson

Turning numbers into useful information

One of the major challenges for the profession is how to handle data and, in particular, how to present the data so that others are able to understand them and thus respond appropriately. Data on clinical care need to be relevant to the clinical teams treating patients, but must also be relevant to managers responsible for organising care and ultimately to users of healthcare. This chapter will refer to two data sets in current use by specialties other than cardiology, and use the response to them to illustrate how the cardiology data sets might develop.

The government White Paper *The new NHS*[1] described the need to 'do the right thing, at the right time, to the right patient and to get it right first time'. This is an attractive sentiment and a laudable aim with which no one can disagree. However, there are problems with this in the real world, beginning with an inability to define what is meant by 'right'? For example, clinicians have adjusted their behaviour over the last few decades. They have learnt to welcome patients to the consultation with a handshake, to talk to patients in clinic, and to explain matters properly – but getting such niceties of behaviour 'right' does not have an effect on the underlying disease. Such behaviour does not help the patient to know whether the doctor has got the diagnosis right or written out the prescription correctly. There are no checks on clinical care at that level. This author (and probably most consultant physicians) has never had any check made on his clinical performance in the outpatient clinic in his entire consultant career.

There are now many well-produced guideline documents that describe best practice. When these first appeared a decade ago, there were lots of excuses as to why they 'might not apply to me'. A common excuse was that doctors as independent practitioners ought to be prepared to act differently for each patient according to his or her individual needs. Clinical governance has changed all that. While doctors still have the right to act on the merits of each individual case, they must also be prepared to justify their reasons for deviating from best practice as set out in the relevant guideline.

Collecting comparative data

The surgeons and anaesthetists set out a way forward by setting up the Confidential Enquiry into Peri-operative Deaths[2]. This began by collecting data confidentially on all deaths following surgical operations. Large discrepancies were found in the results in different hospitals for the same procedure. An important finding was that out-of-hours surgery by junior doctors was associated with a significantly worse outcome. This has led to a major shift in practice to ensure that surgical procedures are performed by more experienced personnel.

However, extrapolating surgical experience to a medical specialty is not easy. In surgery, there is a defined procedure:

- an operation
- a defined end-point: death
- a limited time frame: 30 days.

Medicine is more difficult because it is necessary to consider not single episodes in care over short periods of time but perhaps the outcome of a chronic disease over 20 or 30 years. In the case of acute myocardial infarction, there is an initial sentinel event that can be used to initiate the audit process but the outcome is less easy to define. A number of outcomes could be measured:

- death
- angina, or
- functional status.

– but, in the end, what physicians are working for is to slow the rate of decline of a condition rather than necessarily curing it.

Defining the outcome that should be measured

Thus, the aim of any system attempting to examine the quality of physician care is to devise methods for measuring whether or not the rate of decline has been effectively reduced. It is necessary to work out what data are needed to address the question, to establish that the data are collectable, and that case-mix and other confounders can be controlled. In practice, it is often impossible to collect final outcome data because the results are needed in the present and not five years on. Complete longitudinal data are notoriously difficult to collect. In many situations it is necessary to compromise by collecting process data that have an understood predictive value for outcome: a process-based proxy for outcome. There are several papers that support this approach[3,4]. Confidentiality of audit data remains an issue for some clinicians, but the changing climate in the UK means that it will not be possible in future to conceal data either from NHS management or from the public. Therefore, clinicians setting up audit should consider at the outset how the potential target audiences will want to use the results, and how those results might be expressed. This latter point is important because if it is possible to define the target audience, this will influence the choice of data items to be recorded and the detail (or simplicity) of approach necessary.

The NHS collects a great deal of data on the *quantity* of routine practice, but has little information about the *quality* of practice. The distinction between data and information is that data are numbers, whereas information informs. For data to inform, someone has to interpret, tabulate and organise those data. Perhaps the key feature of the Myocardial Infarction National Audit Project is that John Birkhead and his steering group (which includes clinicians, managers, other professionals, ambulance service personnel and lay persons) are working together to interpret the data. The products of the project must be both seen as robust and recognised as clinically credible before being released to outside bodies for use in planning the NHS cardiology service.

Multicentre audits

The power of multicentre audit studies is the ability to collect data on large numbers of patients. Without big numbers the data are effectively meaningless. Multicentre statistics can detect relatively small differences in process or outcome of care between units with a statistical confidence that the observations are not merely due to chance. These data can be used to set benchmark standards; this will be described in the next section.

Asthma

I first became involved in guidelines and audit via experience in asthma. After the asthma guidelines were published, I was foolish enough to remark that I supposed we ought to know whether the guidelines were working and whether we were changing anything by publishing them. Colleagues agreed, and allocated to me the task of assessing whether there was change.

As part of the asthma audits it became necessary to develop a method for expressing the data so that it would be understandable by a wide audience without needing to revert to league tables[5]. The result was to focus on the box-and-whisker plot. In Fig 1, the data items describe the performance of 36 hospitals for eight separate items of data, each recorded as done or not done for each patient. The median performance for each data item is marked by the square inside the box. The extremes of the box represent the 25th and 75th percentiles of performance, and the extremes of the whiskers reflect the score achieved by the best and the worst hospital for each data item.

Let us consider just one of these eight process measures for the care of acute severe asthma admitted to hospital: whether the patient was given a prescription for inhaled steroids to take home on discharge. There is no argument that, following an acute attack of asthma sufficient to have required hospital admission, it is essential to prescribe the one drug that could prevent the next attack, yet the data show that this was not achieved for 20% of patients. The target is achievable because the upper whisker shows that some hospitals are succeeding 100% of the time. Of greater concern is the hospital at the lowest extreme in which only half the patients are being discharged with the right drug. This is absolutely unacceptable practice, and the hospital or unit deserves to be challenged over this result.

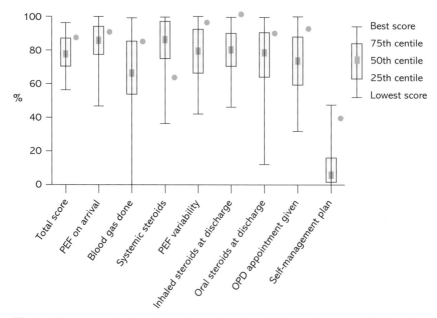

Fig 1. Management of acute asthma. One hospital's performance (●) for eight variables compared with the best, median and worst scores (box-and-whisker plots: see inset) achieved by 36 UK hospitals in the same year. Boxes represent hospital median and interquartile range; whiskers represent extremes of hospital variation (OPD = outpatient department; PEF = peak expiratory flow).

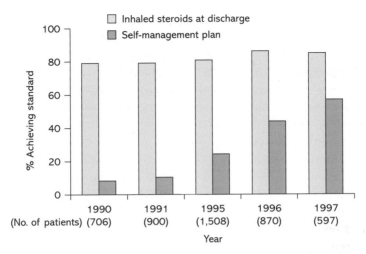

Fig 2. Changes in UK asthma care. Proportion of patients in whom the asthma standard for two of the variables was met over a seven-year period (1990–1997)[7].

The asthma eight-point score is a simplistic assessment of processes of care and its validity as a marker of hospital outcome was questioned by critics. A study in Glasgow[6], which compared the scores achieved by different hospitals with the readmission rates in the next three months, showed that the process score was a predictor of readmission – that is, it was a process-based outcome indicator. This provided support for the professional specialist society to support use of the tool, and to accept that when there is a wide variance between the care of different units (more than 50% variance in this case) it should be investigated.

Audits in asthma have been repeated over a number of years and it has been possible to demonstrate slow but steady change (Fig 2)[7]. Self-management plans, hardly ever used in 1990, are now used in upwards of 60% of cases. It is reasonable to give the patient a written management plan on discharge. While there is still a long way to go towards the target of 100%, it is encouraging that change is occurring. If it is possible to narrow the unacceptably wide variance noted between units for asthma, it should also be possible in other conditions.

Stroke

The stroke audit was conceived as a 'sentinel audit' sponsored by the Department of Health (DoH). This audit went several steps beyond anything achieved by the asthma study. It was launched with a letter to hospital trusts recommending that they should take part. Over 80% responded – it really was a national study. A huge amount of data was collected and, taking advantage of electronic scanning techniques, entered into a computer. Importantly, the questions were piloted, analysed and redesigned so that the quality of data in this study is probably as good as any collected for any audit anywhere[8].

The results have many similarities to the situation for asthma. The questionnaire enquired about several aspects of the process of assessment of the stroke. These have been consolidated into a single variable, which in essence asked the question 'Was the patient properly assessed on arrival?'. The results are set out in Fig 3 for each region of the country using a box-and-whisker plot. The variance between the best and worst hospital is wide in every region (exceeding 70% in some regions); there is an unacceptable variance between good and what can only be described as 'questionable' practice.

Continence care in stroke. The next example looks at the situation for assessment of continence care (Fig 4). The variance between best and worst hospitals is almost 100%. Some hospitals would appear to consider that continence is not an issue for stroke patients. Anyone treating stroke knows that many patients have problems of continence, and it is also an

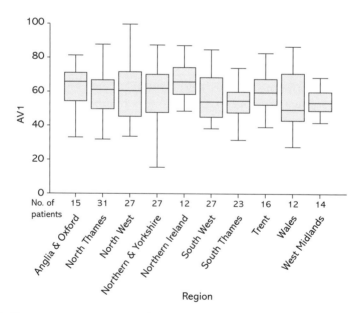

Fig 3. Was proper assessment performed in the first 24 hours? The performance of individual hospitals within each region in performing a correct assessment of the patient on admission. The variable AV1 is an aggregate derived from the 10 measures used to assess the initial patient evaluation[8]. (For explanation of 'boxes and 'whiskers', see Fig 1.)

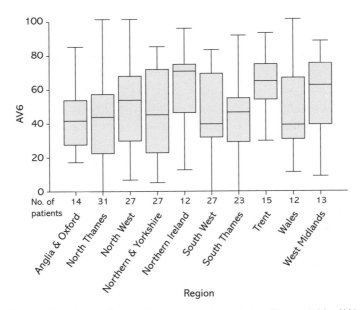

Fig 4. Regional variation in continence care for stroke. The variable AV6 is an aggregate of four measures used to assess continence care. (For explanation of 'boxes' and 'whiskers', see Fig 1.)

issue that many find difficult to discuss. The message from those units that hardly ever attend to continence problems in their patients is worrying. It is a terrible indictment of medicine. No one should be expected to accept such a low standard of care.

Composite variables. One of the important features of the stroke study was that it looked at both the process *and* the organisation of care. If a composite variable of all the process items of care is plotted against a similar composite of the organisation of care, there is a strong correlation across the country (Fig 5). This suggests that there is likely to be a better process leading to a better outcome if care is better organised.

This is an important message. It may not be costly to reorganise, it may require some thought and may require the team to be reorganised. It may sometimes require dysfunctional clinicians to be helped to work together. One of the worse examples was in a hospital where it was known the clinicians did not get on with each other. When the chief executive saw his hospital's data he was galvanised into action and insisted that the clinicians sorted things out. That hospital improved from an overall process score of 23% to 53% in one year and it is understood to be improving further.

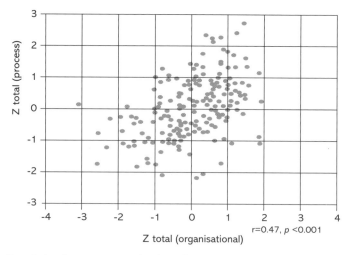

Fig 5. Correlation between organisation of care and process of care. Data are from the sentinel audit of stroke. Z scores are aggregates of all the organisational and process variables used in the study.

Completing the audit loop

It is imperative that if data are collected they are fed back with a full interpretation to the submitting units as quickly as possible. In the asthma studies, data were fed back to the individual units within two months of submission over the duration of the project. However, it took five years to get the professionals to agree that they were happy to be judged on the proxy outcome measure. Overall results were presented to national meetings, but there was no system to make the results specifically relevant locally. Results were not shared with managers since at that time this was not considered proper. Moreover, most chief executives in the early 1990s would not have considered such data as their responsibility.

For the stroke data, the stroke physicians have come on board within a year. They believe these data, are happy to be judged by them, and accept that the people at the bottom need to be investigating their practice. There are several reasons for this acceptance, of which the most important is the high quality of the data and the national coverage, but there was also a huge promulgation exercise. A meeting was held in each region to describe the data to a multidisciplinary group from the participating hospitals, with input from a local champion to describe how his unit or hospital was tackling perceived problems. In this way, the regions could take the results on board and have managed them themselves. For example, in Northern Ireland there is a multidisciplinary stroke interest group looking at their data in an ongoing fashion and really shaking up stroke care. It is a tribute both to the intercollegiate committee that oversaw the national project and to the project team that the results have been set out in such a way that local units should both trust and utilise the data to shape local services.

The stroke audit completed the loop by performing a second round of audit. Comparing years one and two, there was improvement in every aspect of care including organisation of care, initial assessment and secondary prevention (Table 1). The only issue not affected was discharge planning, where it was probably not reasonable to expect links to social services to change in only one year. The changes in one year of the stroke project exceeded what had been achieved in asthma in seven years.

National data collection, high data quality standards, and effective feedback and promulgation do lead to worthwhile changes in care. Many units now speak confidently about their stroke data, and hospitals and others are looking forward to continuing progress. Sadly, neither the DoH (nor its subsidiaries) is providing any continuing funding for this. However, in association with the Stroke Association and others, the Royal College of Physicians has raised funding from other sources to keep the project going.

Who should see and act on the results?

There is a question of who owns the data. As pointed out in earlier chapters, it is not now permissible or appropriate to keep audit data within the clinical professions. Chief executives have a formal duty to deliver clinical governance, and it is their duty to know what our data show our performance to be. The clinical governance support team in Leicester is using the stroke data set as one exemplar to bring about change, getting

Table 1. Changes in stroke care over 12 months. Figures represent a percentage compliance standard for composite measures covering various domains of the care process.

	1998	1999
Organisation of care	55	62
Process:		
initial assessment	58	71
functional assessment	48	57
management planning	52	58
secondary prevention	65	71
discharge planning	63	62

together clinicians, audit facilitators and, most importantly, a board member to work out how their hospital should respond to the data. This is an important step. If the board joins in the exercise, the combined clinical and managerial clout should ensure that action will follow. It is an opportunity clinicians must not miss. It has already been said that many of the failures are actually system failures and not individual human failures. If the clinicians do not have the right facilities, and if the local organisation of services is wrong, they cannot expect to achieve optimum care for patients. Clinicians cannot do it alone.

One of the problems in the past has been that, because nothing was measured, no one was aware of the failings of the service – especially of what was *not* being done. I was involved in helping to write the asthma guidelines, and believed that the service in my hospital was of high quality. However, on analysing the first round of the asthma audit data, it was shown to be in the bottom quartile. It was humbling. On investigation, it was the organisation of care within the unit, within the hospital, and between the accident and emergency department and the wards which had to be addressed. On subsequent studies the hospital has consistently been in the top quartile. Unless there is an objective measurement of the processes of care, deficiencies will not be recognised and therefore will remain uncorrected.

The rationale for these comparative audits is that, unbeknown to us, there are many deficiencies in care. It is not likely that asthma and stroke are the only examples in which there are unacceptable variations between hospitals. Patients deserve better. The aim of all these studies is to do better for patients. As long as that remains the driving force, the next few years should be exciting. Data counting, properly interpreted, should make for a much more interesting environment in which to work. It offers what is probably the most effective way of achieving the aims set out by successive governments, of improving the quality and not just the quantity of care delivered by the NHS.

References

1   Secretary of State for Health. *The new NHS: modern, dependable.* Cm 3807. London: The Stationery Office, 1997.
2   Campling EA, Devlin HB, Hoile RW, Lunn JN. The report of the National Confidential Enquiry into Peri-operative Deaths 1991/2. London: National Confidential Enquiry into Peri-operative Deaths, 1993.
3   Mant J, Hicks N. Detecting differences in quality of care: the sensitivity of measures of process and outcome in treating acute myocardial infarction. *Br Med J* 1995;**311**:793–6.
4   Crombie IK, Davies HT. Beyond health outcomes: the advantages of measuring process. Review. *J Eval Clin Pract* 1998;**4**:31–8.

5   Pearson MG, Ryland I, Harrison BD. National audit of acute severe asthma in adults admitted to hospital. Standards of Care Committee, British Thoracic Society. *Qual Health Care* 1995;**4**:24–30.

6   Slack R, Bucknall CE. Readmission rates are associated with differences in the process of care in acute asthma. *Qual Health Care* 1997;**6**:194–8.

7   Bucknall CE, Ryland I, Cooper A, Coutts I, *et al*. National benchmarking as a support system for clinical governance. *J R Coll Physicians Lond* 2000;**34**:52–6.

8   Gompertz PH, Irwin P, Morris R, Lowe D, *et al*. Reliability and validity of the Intercollegiate Stroke Audit package. *J Eval Clin Pract* 2001;**7**:1–11.

Section Two

Issues specific to acute myocardial infarction

8 | Clinical audit in myocardial infarction: origin and development of the Myocardial Infarction National Audit Project

John Birkhead

This chapter describes the origins and development of the Myocardial Infarction National Audit Project (MINAP). This is an audit of process of management and eventually outcome of myocardial infarction (MI), with which collaborating hospitals will be able to demonstrate their performance in relation to the requirements of the national service framework (NSF) for coronary heart disease[1]. This national audit represents an important collaboration between the MINAP group and colleagues from the Central Cardiac Audit Database (CCAD) who will be responsible for the electronic storage, transmission and analysis of data. The project is sponsored by the National Institute for Clinical Excellence, and it enjoys the support of the NHS Information Authority.

The primary purpose of the audit is twofold:

- to promote high quality care by hospitals, and
- to demonstrate equality of care across the country.

The project also has the potential to allow the fusion of two previously distinct streams of information:

1 Clinical information related to process and outcome of MI.
2 Hospital episode statistical data previously collected by management for the purposes of administration.

Justified concerns have been expressed about the quality of Department of Health (DoH) MI mortality data (league tables) which are derived from data collected by management. MINAP has the potential to improve data quality in both this and other aspects of management of MI. A crucial aspect is to encourage ownership of data by clinicians and, by so doing, persuade them of the validity of analyses subsequently performed on the data. This may not be an easy task in the face of all the other conflicting demands presently required of clinicians but, without the continuing support of clinicians, the work will not succeed.

Initial constraints on collaborative audit

The practice of national collaborative audit has been slow to develop, with the notable exception of the mandatory and long established national perinatal mortality surveys and the more recent confidential enquiries into peri-operative deaths. The several reasons for this may be summarised:

1 Slow and tentative acceptance of clinical audit within the NHS.

2 Absence of a consistent source of funding for national projects.

3 Concerns by clinicians about confidentiality and anonymity of data.

4 Lack of any central (political) impetus to develop collaborative audit.

The NHS and Community Care Act 1990 made clinical audit an obligation and provided audit funds to each hospital trust, which gave an initial impetus to local audit. However, early audit tended to be of the 'snapshot' variety rather than a continuous examination of performance, and the notion of continuous audit was not widely accepted. Nevertheless, it was important at that time to encourage a climate in which audit was accepted as a requirement for all clinicians; a catalyst for this was the initial provision of funds. It was some time before clinicians felt it necessary to look beyond their own hospitals and to compare audit data with other hospitals. Progress was also hampered by the labour-intensive nature of data collection for collaborative audit, although increasingly effective electronic means for data collection and storage have partly reduced the burden. An additional limiting factor was an absence of consistent central funding for collaborative audit. The DoH previously wished to support only pilot projects and required annual application for funding, a time-consuming and frustrating activity.

Initial attempts at collaborative audit were also frustrated by concerns by colleagues about the confidentiality of aggregated or even individual patient data. Concern was twofold, that:

I individual hospitals might be seen by colleagues in other hospitals to be underperforming, and

I clinicians might be criticised by their own management when performance was not thought to be satisfactory.

These concerns were of particular concern at the time of the NHS reforms of 10 years ago when newly gained trust status militated against collaborative work. Thus, the initial collaborative audit which started in 1992 proceeded only on the understanding and trust of colleagues that their hospital data would remain anonymous and available only to clinicians. Over the last 2–3 years the views of clinicians on the need for anonymity have altered – only partly in response to external influence –

to a more open and realistic stance. However, concerns persist about the interpretation of the results of audit. A number of clinical colleagues performing audit of delays in the treatment of patients with MI have expressed concerns within the last year about the difficulties in explaining clinical data to managers who have had access to data which they do not understand[2].

The publication of *The new NHS*[3], and subsequently *The national service framework for coronary heart disease*[1], was crucial to the development of collaborative audit. The former publication stressed the intention of government to improve the quality of medical care and to reduce unacceptable variations in care across the country, while the latter specified the process targets for AMI. The NSF made it clear that the targets were to be monitored by national audit and through the performance management process. This was the direct impetus for the development of MINAP.

Developing audit standards

There was initially some uncertainty about how standards for audit should be developed. In the early 1990s, it was considered that standards could be based on published scientific work or that they might be defined by a national committee[4]. Neither scientific standards nor standards set by a committee are ideal.

Standards based on published scientific work

Audit standards based on published clinical research data, for example the improvement in mortality resulting from the rapid provision of thrombolytic treatment, have to carry the caveat that published scientific data do not always reflect the real world, in terms of the structure of the population studied, the management of patients entered into trials or clinical outcomes.

Standards defined by a national committee

The audit standards for the NSF for coronary heart disease were produced on the advice of an external reference group. It remains to be seen whether a reference standard of 75% eligible patients having thrombolytic treatment within 20 minutes of arrival in hospital is realistic[1].

Comparison with nationally aggregated data

A third proposal is to compare local data with nationally aggregated data[5]. Hospitals in the lower quartile of performance can then aim for the target of the highest quartile. This is the approach being used in the present audit.

Audit of myocardial infarction before the Myocardial Infarction National Audit Project

Collaborative process audit between hospitals in the UK began with a pilot study collecting data from six hospitals over a six-month period[6]. This paper-based study started in 1991 using NCR (no carbon required) forms with central data entry from the forms. Apart from the clinical insights gained, this also provided valuable experience in performing audit of this nature. Following this work, funding was secured via the Research Unit of the Royal College of Physicians to extend the audit to 25 hospitals. A preprogrammed Psion Series 2 organiser was used for data collection and storage and, despite the storage capacity of this electronic system being only 64 Kb, data were recorded on several hundred patients. Data were then transferred electronically to Northampton for statistical analysis using the Statistical Package for the Social Sciences. Paper-based reports were sent to collaborating hospitals every four months. Each hospital had a code number which allowed identification of its own data and comparison with the data of the other hospitals without being able to identify them. This system provided reports within 2–4 weeks of data submission. By 1995, up to 60 hospitals were collaborating, including all the hospitals in the West Midlands Region. Although the prime purpose of the work was to provide colleagues with analyses of performance, the aggregated data also provided valuable information on the provision of care on a wider scale[7,8].

In 1997, with further funding no longer available from the NHS, management of the project was passed to the Clinical Trials Unit of the Royal Brompton Hospital and support was found from pharmaceutical sources. The project became the National Audit of Myocardial Infarction (NAOMI). The data collection and storage became computer-based but continued to provide paper-based reports.

The present project, described in more detail below, is a direct response by the profession to the requirements of the NSF. A core data set of terms relevant to the management of MI has been incorporated into a data application designed to allow clinicians to collect the data required in order to respond to the audit requirements of the NSF. The audit is the outcome of a close collaboration between the MINAP group and CCAD (responsible for the data application, storage, transmission and analysis of data). The CCAD project (described in detail in Chapter 9) allows for the first time online contemporary data analysis, with immediate comparison of local and aggregated national data.

Clinician concerns

The amount of work involved. One of the considerations in developing the national audit was to address the anxiety expressed by clinicians about the amount of work involved in data collection for audit. However, despite advances in information technology, it is accepted that data entry for audit will remain a chore for the foreseeable future. This should be eased, as far as possible, by making data collection part of the routine process of care of the patient. Time wasting activities such as repeated data entry must be prevented by linking data applications to the hospital patient management systems; re-entry of electronic data stored elsewhere in the hospital, such as pharmacy discharge prescriptions, should also be avoided.

Delay between collection and results. Another concern is that delay between data collection and presentation of analyses is often very long, with loss of significance and relevance to clinicians. This has been solved by the MINAP/CCAD collaboration.

Development of a core data set

The development of a core data set for auditing process and outcome of management of AMI was essential for this audit. Data items to be collected should be readily available during routine care of the patient, and ideally kept to a minimum. The initial definitions of the data items used were developed by general consensus over the last decade. In anticipation of the emerging findings of the NSF, a working group was set up towards the end of 1998. This group, which had wide representation from all parts of the profession, selected the core data set based on many of the fields used in previous audits. After considerable refinement, these were published by the working group as the core data set for AMI in 1999[9]. This core data set has been limited to terms which are clear, clinically relevant and supported by robust evidence.

The NHS data dictionary

These definitions have now been included in the NHS data dictionary – an important milestone in the process of merging two previously distinct streams of data collection and a fundamental step in the evolution of the electronic patient record:

- clinical audit data for clinicians, and
- data collection by managers for performance management purposes.

It underlines the importance of this audit, but at the same time raises questions about responsibility for data collection and quality assurance.

Future development of the data set

The core data set is limited to items concerned with the immediate management of AMI. Data items that cannot be ascertained before the patient leaves hospital are not included. The reason for this limitation is that some data items, such as adherence to secondary prevention after discharge, cannot be reliably collected from within hospital. Linking of the audit of initial care with that of events and management after discharge awaits the development of further information technology links between primary and secondary care. The single exception to this is the facility to track patient deaths at any point after discharge using CCAD, the success of which is fundamental to MINAP. Definition of terms directly related to other acute coronary syndromes (eg unstable angina) was intentionally omitted from the initial core data set, but it is intended to remedy this at a future date once the project has become established.

The data set has already had some modification in the light of practical use, and three additional fields were added during 2001. None of these modifications invalidates earlier data. It is anticipated that further limited modification, based on clinical experience with the data set, will take place at infrequent intervals. This is a practical issue related to the need to collaborate with those who provide commercial and other proprietary data applications.

The audit requirements of the national service framework

The initial requirements are that hospitals should be able to demonstrate their success in reaching the targets of the NSF in relation to:

▪ the delays from call for help to treatment for patients with AMI who are eligible for thrombolysis

▪ the provision of secondary prevention measures for all patients with AMI.

Subsequently, hospitals will have to offer data on:

▪ number and percentage of survivors of out-of-hospital arrest

▪ number and age standardised proportion of patients dying within 30 days of a hospital admission with AMI

▪ evidence of documentation of:

– assessment of left ventricular function in discharge communication to the general practitioner (GP)

- arrangements for cardiac rehabilitation in discharge communication to the GP
- results/arrangements for assessing need for revascularisation.

Success of in-hospital resuscitation from cardiac arrest is not specifically mentioned by the NSF, but is recorded in the database as a vitally important indicator of hospital performance.

The MINAP audit responds to the requirements of the NSF outlined above. The audit has two initial strands, continuous and cyclical.

Continuous audit

The first strand is a continuous audit of the immediate management of infarction, to provide evidence of the proportion of eligible patients (ST elevation MI), having reperfusion treatment within defined time limits after a call for help. These data can be collected during the first hours of an admission to hospital. Patients with ST elevation infarction should be admitted to a cardiac care unit, where nurses have shown themselves accurate and enthusiastic at data collection. Nurses doing this work should be appropriately remunerated. MINAP is collaborating with the ambulance service to improve the flow of data generated before admission to hospital, in order to improve data quality on events occurring before admission.

Cyclical audit

There will also be a cyclical audit of all patients with MI, with or without cardiographic ST elevation, to examine the use of secondary prevention measures. It is planned that this should run for three months at 12-month intervals. This work will need the support of audit departments in order to log all patients with infarction who may be cared for in any number of medical wards.

Additional data

In addition, it will be possible from the outset to offer mortality flagging to those hospitals that wish to log all MIs occurring in hospital.

Data validation and quality assurance

It is essential for any audit work that data should be of high quality and that clinicians and management should have confidence in the quality of the raw data so that analyses can be treated with the same confidence.

The project implementation committee has gone to great lengths to achieve this.

To ensure that data entry will conform to agreed definitions we have provided context-sensitive help within the data application:

1 When the data recorder enters a field, *detailed explanations* appear at the side of the box covering all the options available for that field. This prevents different recorders having idiosyncratic interpretations of data responses.

2 *Error checking* routines have been incorporated within the data application to prevent the entry of obviously erratic data, particularly in relation to the timing of events.

3 A set of *application notes* has also been written, providing detailed help on data completion in different sets of clinical circumstances.

4 For *further advice* about data entry, a help desk is provided for clinical questions (manned 9 am–5 pm throughout the week).

We suggest that 5% of all clinical records (ca 15–30) should be audited annually for accuracy of data entry in each hospital. This will involve hospital audit departments examining the notes and data entry forms and comparing the data with that entered into the data application. A sample of about 20 of the data fields will be used. Audit departments will return a completed assessment form and hospitals given a rating for data accuracy. Once data entry has taken place, the completeness of the data can be examined by CCAD who will provide online analyses of data quality. The 'sanity' of the data can also be examined by CCAD. (See Chapters 9 and 12 for further discussion on data validation and data analysis.)

Sanctions

It is not the remit of the MINAP group to enforce audit, but rather to offer support for those who have to engage in this work as part of their response to the NSF. It is vital, however, to ensure as far as possible that data quality is high, as national data will be derived from the analyses. It is to be expected that overall data quality and completeness will be high, but where there is evidence of poor quality *data*, as opposed to evidence of poor quality *care*, hospitals will be advised of their position and, if necessary, external validation imposed.

References

1   Department of Health. *National service framework for coronary heart disease: modern standards of care and service models.* London: DoH, 2000.

2   Birkhead J. A baseline survey of facilities for the management of acute myocardial infarction in England 2000. London: Royal College of Physicians, 2001.

3   Department of Health. *The new NHS: modern, dependable.* Cmd 3807. London: The Stationery Office, 1997.

4   Hampton JR. Problems with audit of coronary surgery and angioplasty. *Hospital Update* 1992;**18**:23–6.

5   Birkhead JS. Minimum data sets for angina: a necessary basis for audit. In: de Bono D, Hopkins A (eds). *Management of stable angina.* London: Royal College of Physicians, 1994:133–41.

6   Birkhead JS. Time delays in provision of thrombolytic treatment in six district hospitals. Joint Audit Committee of the British Cardiac Society and a Cardiology Committee of Royal College of Physicians of London. *Br Med J* 1992;**305**:445–8.

7   Birkhead JS. Thrombolytic treatment for myocardial infarction: an examination of practice in 39 United Kingdom hospitals. Myocardial Infarction Audit Group. *Heart* 1997;**78**:28–33.

8   Birkhead JS. Trends in the provision of thrombolytic treatment between 1993 and 1997. Myocardial Infarction Audit Group. *Heart* 1999;**82**:438–42.

9   Birkhead JS, Norris RM, Quinn T, Pearson M. Acute myocardial infarction: a core data set for monitoring standards of care. London: Royal College of Physicians, 1999.

9 | Role of the Central Cardiac Audit Database in the audit of myocardial infarction

David Cunningham, Anthony Rickards and Carol Westland

Cardiovascular disease causes more premature mortality and morbidity in developed countries than any other organ disease[1,2]. A massive evidence base now exists for the principal treatments of common conditions; this allows a definition of optimal management to be made, usually referred to as clinical guidelines. There is, of course, an assumption by both doctor and patient that the application of agreed clinical guidelines to an individual patient will result in the outcome defined by the prior evidence base. Too rarely is the outcome actually measured[3,4].

Clinical audit

Clinical audit may be defined in a number of ways. At its simplest, it is application of the pooled findings of clinical trials to all medical practice, with the requirement to define the patient, disease, treatment and outcome in a way that can be used to compare results against contemporary evidence.

Clinical audit may also be seen in the context of quality assurance, where it is but one element of a process which enables the identification of both good and bad practice and results in discussion, debate and action to improve practice globally. The failure of the audit process in the Bristol Cardiothoracic unit[5], the subsequent pronouncements of the Secretary of State for Health[6] and the NHS information strategy[7] make abundantly clear our individual and institutional responsibilities.

This chapter discusses the requirements of an audit system for acute myocardial infarction (AMI) and acute coronary syndromes in general, but the principles apply equally to other clinical areas. The illustrations are taken from a hospital which is part of the Myocardial Infarction National Audit Project (MINAP)[8], run jointly by the Clinical Effectiveness and Evaluation Unit of the Royal College of Physicians of London and the Central Cardiac Audit Database (CCAD)[9].

Until the inception of the CCAD project, a single cardiac centre had limited ability to collect audit data capable of meaningful analysis. There are many local examples of good record keeping, but there are several limitations of such an approach for audit:

1 Most centres do not have enough patients with the same disease and risk factors. Internal analysis, for example of performance by time or by type of treatment, results in wide confidence intervals. This is the case despite the use of statistical techniques such as cumulative sum and variable life-adjusted delay analyses[10,11] designed to identify trends from small numbers of procedures. Statistically, it is unlikely that useful information for audit can be generated.

2 Even when a centre treats large numbers of the 'same' patients with the 'same' therapy, comparison with other centres or with the established literature is compromised by the definition of the patient population which cannot be standardised in a purely local database.

3 In general, local centres do not have the time and resources to record patient outcome after leaving hospital following an index event. Centralised tracking can identify late outcomes.

4 Most hospitals are comfortable with providing annual anonymised summaries of activity, but such information is essentially useless in determining performance based on patient outcome. Centres are naturally concerned about providing patient-specific data when both patient and medical staff confidentiality may be put at risk. A secure system is needed.

All these issues have been important in limiting the good intentions of clinicians to take part in effective audit; they can be solved only by the sort of solutions offered by CCAD. Data can be contributed whilst preserving the security of access to patient and staff identification. Definitions of procedures and patient populations can be generated to allow meaningful analysis.

Medical quality assurance

Medical quality assurance starts with the definition of a domain of interest for clinical audit, during which a decision has to be made about where to 'start' the process. The domain we will discuss is AMI, so the starting point appears easy to define: admission to hospital. However, as often the case with audit, there are exceptions to every rule: for instance, a patient admitted for an unrelated condition may infarct in hospital, in which case the starting point cannot be the patient's admission to hospital. The ideal starting point is the onset of symptoms or, if this cannot be established, the time when the patient first called for help.

Data definition

The definition of the data to be collected for audit should be considered under several categories.

Structure. One set of data is concerned with defining the environment in which treatment is being delivered and the quality of the data collected. It should provide adequate information to answer the question whether a particular form of treatment should be delivered in a specific environment. Some 'fixed' variables defining the institutional facilities which need to be collected and collated on a regular basis for comparisons against defined standards are:

▪ the name of the hospital
▪ whether it is in an urban or a rural setting, and
▪ the numbers of consultant cardiologists and junior medical staff.

Other fixed variables are:

▪ numbers of patients admitted to the coronary care unit in one year
▪ whether or not thrombolytic treatment is given in the accident and emergency department, and
▪ whether or not there is a catheter laboratory.

Figure 1, from an online patient database, shows the completeness of individual patient-based data items from which are derived indices of quality of care. The analysis compares the local hospital (Your Hospital) with the national average (All Other Hospitals). The local data inspection shows that the overall data completeness is lower in Your Hospital, in large part due to an absence of admission route local data. Such a display can quickly illustrate to local users the deficiencies in their data and allow them to address and correct them. An institution may have the appropriate facilities but cannot provide the basics of quality assurance without meeting standards of data collection.

Data completeness	N	Overall	DoB	NHS Number	Postcode	Ethnic	Adm Dx	Final Dx	Adm route	Adm date
All Other Hospitals	4,563	87.8%	96.5%	67.4%	90.7%	100.0%	98.6%	88.9%	85.9%	99.1%
Your Hospital	140	74.3%	99.3%	74.3%	93.6%	100.0%	77.1%	99.1%	0.0%	100.0%
	4,703	87.5%	96.6%	67.6%	90.8%	100.0%	97.9%	89.2%	83.3%	99.1%

Fig 1. Data completeness analysis for acute myocardial infarction (Adm = admission; DOB = date of birth; DX = diagnosis).

Appropriateness. Another set of data asks whether it was appropriate that a particular form of treatment was delivered to a particular patient. Appropriateness may be considered both as:

Hospital	Final Diagnosis	Admission Diagnosis	N
All other hospitals			
	Definite myocardial infarction		5796
		Chest pain of uncertain cause	575
		Definite myocardial infarction	3295
		Other admission diagnosis	367
		Probable myocardial infarction	872
		Unstable angina	687
Your hospital			
	Definite myocardial infarction		202
		Chest pain of uncertain cause	4
		Definite myocardial infarction	119
		Other admission diagnosis	51
		Unstable angina	28

Fig 2. Admission diagnosis of definite myocardial infarction as a proportion of all infarctions.

▌ indications for treatment (eg severity of symptoms), and

▌ contraindications (eg in the case of thrombolytic treatment, uncontrolled hypertension or risk of haemorrhage).

Definition of the appropriateness variables is a key step in clinical audit as it will allow comparison of the results of treatment in different institutions in similar groups of patients.

Figure 2 shows the number of AMIs admitted to the local hospital compared with the rest of the country. The local hospital reported 119 cases diagnosed as definite MI on admission and 202 on discharge (59%), compared with the national data which shows 3,295 versus 5,796 (57%). If this difference were significant, there would be a possible reporting bias and the local hospital might consider reviewing its inclusion criteria.

'Drilling down' into the data permits more detail to be displayed for selected groups of records. In Fig 3, local and national reasons for not giving thrombolytic treatment (as registered by the centres) are shown in patients with an admission diagnosis of definite MI. Nationally, in 216 of 1,371 patients (16%) there was a reason for not giving treatment. Locally, 12 out of 145 patients (8%) had a valid reason. There is therefore no reason to suspect that this local hospital is using the 'reasons for not giving ...' field to camouflage poor performance in delivering thrombolytic therapy.

Central quality control of data will look at figures such as the percentage of patients classified as having a valid reason for not getting treatment. If the percentage appears significantly higher than in other hospitals, queries will be raised with the hospital.

Demographics	Admission Diagnosis	Therapy Contraindications	N
All Other Hospitals			
	definite MI	none	1155
		Administrative failure	4
		Elective decision	29
		Ineligible ECG	45
		Risk of haemorrhage	42
		Too late	95
		Uncontrolled hypertension	1
Your Hospital			
	definite MI	none	133
		Administrative failure	4
		Elective decision	4
		Risk of haemorrhage	1
		Too late	3

Fig 3. Reasons for not giving thrombolytic treatment (MI = myocardial infarction).

Process. The next set of data defines the process by which treatment was delivered (in this case thrombolytic treatment). It includes important benchmark data such as:

▪ call-to-hospital time

▪ door-to-needle time, and

▪ the percentage of eligible patients who receive therapy.

The upper panel of Fig 4 shows call-to-hospital time ('ambulance time'). The national average is 66 minutes, compared with 58 minutes locally. The percentage of patients who reach hospital in under 30 minutes is 19% nationally and 28% locally. Before any local complacency creeps in, the national service framework (NSF) for coronary heart disease benchmark suggests that 75% of patients who are eligible for thrombolysis should reach hospital in under 30 minutes[12].

The lower panel shows a similar display for hospital-to-treatment time ('door-to-needle time'). Again, local performance is slightly better than national, with 48% receiving treatment within 30 minutes of arrival compared with a national average of 35%, but both figures fall well short of the benchmark of 75%.

Call for help to Arrival at Hospital	N	Call to hospital time (mins)	% < 30 minutes	% < 60 minutes	
All Other Hospitals	2440	65.8	18.6%	68.0%	
Your Hospital	143	58.2	28.0%	76.2%	
Arrival at Hospital to Reperfusion Treatment	N	Door to needle (mins)	< = 30 min	< = 60 min	< = 120 min
All Other Hospitals	1159	64.8	34.8%	71.1%	89.6%
Your Hospital	127	54.5	48.0%	73.2%	93.7%

Fig 4. Call-to-hospital and hospital-to-treatment times.

Figure 5 illustrates another measure of process, namely the percentage of patients treated who are eligible for thrombolytic treatment. Nationally, 79% of patients eligible for treatment get treated compared with 88% locally. Treatment is virtually always by thrombolytic drug – only two of 1,300 patients had an acute interventional procedure (percutaneous transluminal coronary angioplasty).

Definite MI	Therapy	N	Reperfused	(%)
▼ All other hospitals		1689	1329	78.7%
	1. Thrombolytic drug	1281	1281	
	2. PTCA	2	2	
	3. Not attempted	273	0	
	4. Method unknown	133	46	
▼ Your hospital		145	128	88.3%
	1. Thrombolytic drug	128	128	
	3. Not attempted	13	0	
	4. Method unknown	4	0	

Fig 5. Proportion of eligible patients receiving thrombolytic treatment (PTCA = percutaneous transluminal angioplasty).

Use of secondary prevention. Another process measure defined by the NSF is the use of secondary prevention measures such as drug therapy with aspirin, beta-blockers, angiotensin-converting enzyme inhibitors and statins. Fig 6 shows the prescriptions of aspirin on discharge: 99% of local and 93% of national patients are on aspirin at discharge, comfortably exceeding the benchmark figure of 75%.

Hospital	Admissions	Aspirin at discharge?
All Other Hospitals	1986	92.8%
Your Hospital	86	98.8%

Fig 6. Prescriptions of aspirin at discharge from hospital.

Outcomes. Any therapy should be associated with well-defined desired and undesired outcomes. These will include key clinical and quality of life variables such as mortality, but could also include resource oriented information such as time off work. Comparisons of mortality figures have potential pitfalls (see Chapters 2, 3 and 13), and strategies for reporting by MINAP are still under discussion. For the present, MINAP is concentrating on the structure, appropriateness and process matters described above.

Data security

In implementing a data collection system, an institution must be aware of its responsibility to protect both patients and healthcare professionals without compromising the objective of audit. In a review commissioned by the British Medical Association, Anderson laid down the principles of data security and confidentiality[13] (listed in brief in Table 1).

Table 1.

1	All records in a database must contain an 'access control list' which determines who can add to, read or edit the information in that record.
2	Records cannot be deleted.
3	All record access for addition or modification of data is both time stamped and electronically signed by the user.
4	All information within the database, whether stored or transmitted, is encrypted.
5	There is a 'trusted authority' that issues and revokes encryption/decryption keys to individual users.
6	Institutions have an encryption key with which access to the patient and physician identifiers can be limited to users defined by that institution.
7	Access to anonymised aggregated information is limited and determined as a matter of policy by the institution.

Summary

The CCAD project has been set up to harmonise a variety of contemporary data collection exercises in cardiovascular medicine. It has applied the techniques of medical quality assurance in utilising a data set defined by the medical domain of interest, and has categorised the analysis of these data in terms of structure, appropriateness, process and outcome (clinical audit's where, when, why, who and what happened). This chapter describes the implementation of such a system in AMI in a single institution, and sets a standard for intra- and interinstitutional medical quality assurance.

References

1 Weinstein MC, Stason WB. Cost-effectiveness of interventions to prevent or treat coronary heart disease. *Annu Rev Public Health* 1985;**6**:41–63.
2 Drummond MF. Survey of cost-effectiveness and cost-benefit analyses in industrialized countries. *World Health Stat Q* 1985;**38**:383–401.
3 Hampton JR. The need for standards for audit of coronary surgery and angioplasty. Review. *Curr Opin Cardiol* 1991;**6**:912–7.
4 Brennecke R, Kadel C. Requirements for quality assessment in coronary angiography and angioplasty. Review. *Eur Heart J* 1995;**16**:1578–88.
5 The Bristol cardiac babies. http://news2.thdo.bbc.co.uk/hi/english/health/background_briefings/the_bristol_heart_babies/
6 Statement by the Secretary of State for Health. http://ccad3.biomed.gla.ac.uk/ccad/frank.htm

7   Information for Health: an information strategy for the modern NHS. http://www.doh.gov.uk/nhsexipu/strategy/index.htm

8   Birkhead JS, Norris R, Quinn T, Pearson M. Acute myocardial infarction: a core dataset for monitoring standards of care. London: Royal College of Physicians, 1999.

9   Rickards A, Cunningham AD. From quantity to quality: the central cardiac audit database project. Review. *Heart* 1999;**82**(Suppl 2):II18–22.

10 de Laval MR, Francois K, Bull C, Brawn W, Spiegelhalter D. Analysis of a cluster of surgical failures. Application to a series of neonatal arterial switch operations. *J Thorac Cardiovasc Surg* 1994;**107**:914-23; discussion 923–4.

11 Lovegrove J, Valencia O, Treasure T, Sherlaw-Johnson, Gallivan S. Monitoring the results of cardiac surgery by variable life-adjusted display. *Lancet* 1997;**350**:1128–30.

12 Department of Health. *National service framework for coronary heart disease: modern standards of care and service models.* London: DoH, 2000.

13 Anderson R. Clinical system security: interim guidelines. *Br Med J* 1996;**312**:109–11.

10 | Collaboration and teamwork with data collection: the nurse's role

Deborah Hughes

The role of the nurse in cardiac care has evolved considerably since the introduction of the coronary care unit (CCU) in the 1960s. The acute care role has grown to encompass the further technical innovations of the 1970s and 1980s, but the cardiac nurse of today has also developed a role in primary care, preventive strategies, chronic disease management, rehabilitation, research and audit. It is clear that cardiac services cannot progress without a strong and co-ordinated nursing workforce, working closely with the rest of the multidisciplinary team.

The nurse-doctor relationship

In the past, the nurse-doctor relationship has been somewhat tenuous and unsettled. Stein's classic paper of 1967[1] on the 'doctor-nurse game' explored the way in which nurses would not undermine the dominance of the medical profession by displaying their own expert opinions and knowledge. When Stein revisited this work in 1990[2] it was noted that relationships had reached a more equal footing, characterised by different but equally valued contributions to decision making. This does not mean that everything in the garden is rosy: working together can still be difficult and problematic. Nurses are often viewed as needing to assert their professional knowledge, experience and assurance in the face of medical power, whilst doctors are considered to be assured of a naturally dominant place by virtue of their medical training.

Collaboration and teamwork

It is clear that both a greater amount of collaboration and the development of closer teamwork are essential if we wish to achieve the optimum therapeutic environment for our patients. Collaboration involves the sharing of responsibilities for solving problems and making decisions in order to formulate and carry out plans. It demands that participants co-operate and show concern for another person's interest, and also requires individuals to be assertive and concerned for their own interest. Characteristics of good teamworking should include the encouragement of maximum participation by all who have something to offer, whilst removing hierarchies from the care system. The emphasis should be on broadening each team member's vision of all services offered by the organisation and on promoting continuity and co-ordination of services, as discussed by Hamilton[3]. If, because of good collaboration, all participants in the team are able to work at an optimal level, patient care should improve.

The advanced nurse role

The emergence of the advanced nurse role in its many guises took place in the UK during the 1980s. The Cumberlege Report in 1986[4] highlighted as positive developments roles such as nurse practitioners and nurse specialists. These were mainly in primary care and enjoyed the benefits of the 1987 White Paper *Promoting better health*[5], which saw the focus of healthcare delivery as being in primary care with the general practitioner at its epicentre. Changing roles were further influenced by factors such as the Calman Report[6], and the change in junior doctors' hours.

The advanced role of the nurse has emerged rapidly and demands appear to be high. The nurse must therefore question the part nursing plays within the overall picture, and accept responsibility for areas never before deemed to be within the nursing role. Certainly, areas such as data collection and audit have always been seen as the responsibility of somebody else. The need for clinical staff to take an active part in reviewing the quality of services they provide and in planning ways of improving them has never had a higher profile within the NHS.

Clinical audit

Clinical audit criteria have been identified to enable staff to monitor the effectiveness of the services they deliver. These tools may be used to identify and share strengths in the service, and also to highlight weaknesses and gaps in order that we may develop strategies to address them. Nurses are in a prime position to collect information in a prospective manner, thereby performing a leading role in shaping the service. In the past, audit and performance indicators have been criticised for focusing on the volume and cost of an activity without giving sufficient emphasis to the more qualitative aspects of appropriateness, effectiveness and quality. These aspects are identical to the areas on which most nursing research has focused.

My own experience of data collection has been laborious, inefficient and frustrating. It has involved the need to trawl through hundreds of sets of notes to find a limited amount of data which has often been poorly recorded and of dubious reliability. The task of identifying my inadequate experience to perform retrospective data collection has unlocked for me the mystery of audit. Despite the trauma of the undertaking, the outcome was worth the effort. By identifying an area in which the service was lacking, I was able to develop an innovative strategy to address the need: that is, the introduction of a nurse specialist role for the management of the patient with acute myocardial infarction (AMI).

Electronic data recording

The opportunity to record data electronically, prospectively and online has now revolutionised the concept of audit. No longer will it be necessary to examine hundreds of sets of notes to record data of doubtful reliability. The reliability will now be increasingly the responsibility of the person recording the data, and should be enhanced by the data recorded being close to the event and fresh in the mind – not weeks, months or years old.

The reality, however, is that data collection and audit may be time-consuming, and critics may say that nurses should use their clinical skills by the bedside rather than at computer terminals. It is particularly important to consider these views in the light of the current situation regarding nursing shortages with increased staff turnover. In this climate of specialisation and expanded roles, nurses are moving into areas traditionally considered to be the remit of doctors. Twenty years ago ECG recordings were performed only by doctors. Now we have nurses involved with history taking and triage, and commencing therapies such as the administration of thrombolysis entirely without the input of medical colleagues. As nurses are willing to take on dynamic medical roles, they must also be willing to take on the more mundane tasks of data collection and audit.

Nurse involvement in audit

The government, as laid down in the national service framework (NSF) for coronary heart disease[7], expects all doctors and clinical teams to take part in clinical audit. This provides nurses with another area for close collaboration with the multidisciplinary team. Nurses spend more time with patients than any other healthcare professional and are therefore in the best position to collect reliable and relevant information. Moreover, a coronary care nurse who has had months or years of training and experience in caring for patients with AMI may be in a better position to judge the quality of data than a house physician or senior house officer on a six-month rotation. The importance of accurately recorded information in the shaping of future services cannot be overestimated, and can only lead to a further forging together of the principles of teamwork. Nurses should see audit as an important and intrinsic part of their role. This is their chance to inform the service as opposed to being informed by it. It is important for nurses to identify the benefits which they may gain from being involved in audit.

The Myocardial Infarction National Audit Project

The importance of the role of the nurse in the smooth running of data collection is recognised in the Myocardial Infarction National Audit Project (MINAP)[8]. MINAP focuses on patients with AMI, so the task of data collection will fall mainly on the CCU nurse. CCU nurses have already demonstrated in many studies their proactive skills and enthusiasm for data collection and input, and are well-known for their accuracy in clinical record keeping. Prospective audit data will already be available in areas such as door-to-needle times – an area in which many nurses are developing responsible roles in response to identified needs. MINAP also collects data regarding secondary prevention issues such as cholesterol screening, evidence-based drug administration, and the provision of rehabilitation services. Identification of inadequate provision relating to these areas may be a further important service.

National service frameworks

An NSF for care of the elderly has been published and one for diabetes is in preparation. Implementation of each framework will require audit. Nursing involvement in data collection relating to these frameworks will enhance collaborative teamwork and ensure that nurses are involved with the shaping of future services to benefit patients.

Conclusion

The terms teamwork, collaboration, leadership, ownership and empowerment frequently appear in NHS communications[9]. They are often considered to be no more than 'management-speak', overused and meaningless, yet they are important words whose meaning must become an intrinsic part of the nursing role if patient-centred care and the clinical governance agenda are to succeed. The challenge is to turn 'management-speak' into action. The workforce is the greatest asset of the NHS. By working together across the board, improvements will be achieved.

References

1   Stein LI. The doctor-nurse game. *Arch Gen Psychiatry* 1967;**16**:699–703.

2   Stein LI, Watts DT, Howell T. The doctor-nurse game revisited. *N Engl J Med* 1990;**322**:546–9.

3   Hamilton J. Toppling the power of the pyramid. Team-based restructuring for TQM, patient-centred care. *Hospitals* 1993;**67**:38,40–1.

4   Cumberlege J. *Neighbourhood nursing: a focus for care.* London: Department of Health and Social Security, 1986.

5   Department of Health and Social Security. *Promoting better health: the government's programme for improving primary health care.* London: Her Majesty's Stationery Office, 1987.

6   Calman C. *Hospital doctors: training for the future. The report of the working group on specialist medical training.* London. Department of Health, 1993.

7   Department of Health. *National service framework for coronary heart disease: modern standards and service models.* London: DoH, 2000.

8   Birkhead JS, Norris RM, Quinn T, Pearson M. *Acute myocardial infarction: a core data set for monitoring standards of care.* London: Royal College of Physicians, 1999.

9   An agenda for change. *NHS Magazine Opinion.* April 2001:24.

11 | Auditing the pre-hospital phase of myocardial infarction

Robin Norris

Acute coronary deaths outside hospital

Two-thirds or more of acute coronary deaths occur outside hospital[1], and in people under 55 years of age the proportion is greater than 90%[2]. Clearly, the greatest potential for reduction in fatality rates lies in the pre-hospital phase of infarction. The concept of pre-hospital coronary care was introduced by Pantridge in Belfast in 1968[3] and has been most successfully applied in King County, Washington, USA[4]. In England, diagnosis, life support and defibrillation were first performed by ambulance personnel in Brighton in the early 1970s[5], and it has been calculated[6] that results in Brighton during the 1980s[7] were comparable with the best of those in the USA (8–9 lives saved per 100,000 of the population per year). Currently in the UK only 6–7% of victims of unexpected but witnessed cardiac arrest occurring outside hospital are successfully resuscitated and discharged from hospital[2,8], but the absolute numbers of survivors from this most common fatal condition are substantial. It was estimated that the total fatality rate of heart attack in the community had been reduced from 46.5% to 45% by resuscitation from cardiac arrest[2]. Recent surveys in UK hospitals[9,10] show that 35–40% of patients with cardiac arrest who were successfully resuscitated and discharged from hospital had their first arrest outside hospital, and so owed their lives to the ambulance service.

Access to a defibrillator

The major obstacle to implementation of the chain of survival[11] from out-of-hospital arrest is delay in access to a defibrillator. Success is enhanced if basic life support is started by relatives or bystanders who have witnessed the arrest. Campaigns to educate the public in life support have been carried out in many parts of the world[12,13] and have been shown to improve survival. Public access defibrillation[14] is a further development which may improve the chance of survival. In cases of out-of-hospital arrest not witnessed by ambulance personnel, accurate audit of the pre-hospital phase of infarction necessitates recording whether or not bystander resuscitation was carried out before arrival of the ambulance and whether or not defibrillation by a member of the public had been attempted.

Audit of the pre-hospital phase

How can the pre-hospital phase be audited in the Myocardial Infarction National Audit Project (MINAP)? Some audit of the chain of survival will be possible in MINAP because it includes all patients arriving at hospital with an unassisted cardiac output following an out-of-hospital arrest. Such patients have been shown to comprise about 5% of all patients admitted with infarction[9,10], and about half of these patients survive to be discharged from hospital[9,15].

If the proportion of patients admitted following out-of-hospital arrest falls much below 5%, and this has been shown to be unlikely due to the play of chance, there are three possible reasons:

1 Local members of the public are not calling the ambulance quickly enough.

2 The hospital concerned is perceived by the ambulance service as difficult to access so that critically ill patients are taken to another nearby hospital.

3 The ambulance service may be inadequately performing advanced life support. If this possibility can be shown to be the most likely reason, problems may need to be addressed.

Apart from this measure of outcome, indices of process for hospital treated patients will also be audited by MINAP. Implementation of the prescribed target of an eight-minute response time for calls for chest pain[16] will be monitored. Both for 999 calls and for calls to general practitioners (GPs), times of call for help and arrival of the emergency service at home and at the hospital will be recorded and delays calculated. Increased delay is of course inevitable if the patient initially calls his or her GP rather than the emergency service. GPs who subsequently call for an ambulance are now in most services having their calls automatically upgraded from a category B call (for which the target time is one hour) to a category A 999 emergency call. In the future, thrombolytic treatment may be initiated by paramedics, which the MINAP database can also accommodate.

The above aggregated data will of course be available to ambulance services. However, the amount of information will almost certainly be inadequate fully to inform review of performance and planning for improvement. As far as resuscitation is concerned, no record will be provided of failed attempts, the proportion of victims of sudden cardiac death in whom resuscitation was attempted by the ambulance, or those on whom basic life support had been attempted by bystanders.

Further audit of ambulance performance

It is highly desirable that further audit of ambulance performance should be compatible with MINAP, and that the ambulance service should have a sense of partnership with the project. How can this be achieved?

Historically, ambulance services have for many years audited their performance, but the audit process usually stopped abruptly once the patient reached hospital. Thus, successful out-of-hospital resuscitations have been monitored, but there has been no way of knowing whether a patient surviving out-of-hospital arrest had died in hospital or survived to be discharged. These problems have been overcome to a certain extent in a recent audit carried out in the South-Eastern region of the UK over one year (1999–2000) by the South-East Ambulance Clinical Audit Group (SEACAG)[17]. This survey showed that the biggest obstacles to monitoring outcomes in a collaborative way were differing definitions and calculations of survival. However, reliable data were obtained from three ambulance services over the year on numbers of patients resuscitated and discharged from hospital.

The opportunity now exists for a seamless audit, and the Joint Royal Colleges Ambulance Liaison Committee (JRCALC), the Ambulance Services Association National Clinical Effectiveness Programme (ASANCEP) and SEACAG are collaborating with the MINAP team with this objective.

Specifically, ambulance services in the UK are required to audit the proportion of category A (emergency 999) calls which are attended within eight minutes by a trained individual with a defibrillator. They must also record the numbers and proportions of patients eligible for thrombolytic treatment who arrive at hospital within 30 minutes of a call for professional help.

With the inclusion of a unique identifier specified by the ambulance service, the MINAP core data set will enable cross-referencing of hospital and ambulance data. The potential for providing linkage between the pre- and in-hospital stages of care has been discussed with representatives from SEACAG which is developing a data set from the pre-hospital phase with particular reference to treatment given before arrival at hospital. Such treatment may in the future include pre-hospital administration of a thrombolytic drug.

The SEACAG database aims to provide data for research and clinical audit which will facilitate the provision of information about structure, process and outcome. By collecting the ambulance identifier, the MINAP database will be able to provide aggregate information about in-hospital diagnosis and treatment. This will allow for retrospective audit of ambulance data, including all cases of cardiac arrest where resuscitation was attempted and possibly, after an appropriate evaluation of feasibility, all patients with chest pain thought to be cardiac in origin.

These clinical audit goals will be enhanced by individualised ambulance connections to the Central Cardiac Audit Database central servers to access relevant data online. These audit developments are part of a commitment shared jointly by SEACAG, JRCALC and MINAP to collect and report high quality data that are accepted as credible by all who use them.

Acknowledgements

I am grateful to Lesley Cave, Director of the SEACAG and Andrew Georgiou, Coronary Heart Disease Programme Co-ordinator, Clinical Evaluation and Effectiveness Unit, Royal College of Physicians, for help with writing this chapter.

References

1 Tunstall-Pedoe H, Kuulasmaa K, Amouyel P, Arrveiler D, *et al.* Myocardial infarction and coronary deaths in the World Health Organization MONICA Project. Registration procedures, event rates, and case-fatality rates in 38 populations from 21 countries in four continents. *Circulation* 1994;**90**:583–612.

2 Norris RM. Fatality outside hospital from acute coronary events in three British health districts 1994–5. United Kingdom Heart Attack Study Collaborative Group. *Br Med J* 1998;**316**:1065–70.

3 Pantridge JF, Geddes JS. A mobile intensive-care unit in the management of myocardial infarction. *Lancet* 1967;**ii**:271–3.

4 Cobb LA, Weaver WD, Fahrenbruch CE, Hallstrom AP, Copass MK. Community-based intervention for sudden cardiac death. Impact, limitations, and changes. *Circulation* 1992;**85**(1 Suppl):I98–102.

5 White NM, Parker WS, Binning RA, Kimber ER, *et al.* Mobile coronary care provided by ambulance personnel. *Br Med J* 1973;**3**:618–22.

6 Norris RM. *Sudden cardiac death and acute myocardial infarction in three British health districts: the UK Heart Attack Study.* London: British Heart Foundation, 1999.

7 Lewis SJ, Holmberg S, Quinn E, Baker K, *et al.* Out-of-hospital resuscitation in East Sussex 1981 to 1989. *Br Heart J* 1993;**70**:568–73.

8 Pell JP, Sirel JM, Marsden AK, Ford I, Cobbe SM. Effect of reducing ambulance response times on deaths from out of hospital cardiac arrest: cohort study. *Br Med J* 2001;**322**:1385–8.

9 Effect of time from onset to coming under care on fatality of patients with acute myocardial infarction: effect of resuscitation and thrombolytic treatment. The

United Kingdom Heart Attack Study (UKHAS) Collaborative Group. *Heart* 1998;**80**:114–20.

10   Norris RM. A new performance indicator for acute myocardial infarction. *Heart* 2001;**85**:395–401.

11   Cummins RO, Ornato JP, Thies WH, Pepe PE. Improving survival from sudden cardiac arrest: the 'chain of survival' concept. A statement for health professionals from the Advanced Cardiac Life Support Subcommittee and the Emergency Cardiac Care Committee, American Heart Association. Review. *Circulation* 1991;**83**:1832–47.

12   Vincent R, Martin B, Williams G, Quinn E, *et al.* A community training scheme in cardiopulmonary resuscitation. *Br Med J* 1984;**288**:617–20.

13   Thompson RG, Hallstrom AP, Cobb LA. Bystander-initiated cardiopulmonary resuscitation in the management of ventricular fibrillation. *Ann Intern Med* 1979;**90**:737–40.

14   Gratton M, Lindholm DJ, Campbell JP. Public-access defibrillation: where do we place the AEDs? *Prehosp Emerg Care* 1999;**3**:303–5.

15   Grubb NR, Elton RA, Fox KA. In-hospital mortality after out-of-hospital cardiac arrest. *Lancet* 1995;**346**:417–21.

16   NHS Executive. *Review of ambulance performance standards: final report of the steering group.* London: Department of Health, 1996.

17   Cave DL. *Variation of recording prehospital cardiac arrest survival in UK ambulance trusts.* MSc thesis, University of Westminster, 2000.

The critical importance of data quality in the monitoring of healthcare: mechanisms for ensuring robustness and accuracy

Andrew Georgiou, Louise Knight and Lynne Walker

The importance of monitoring healthcare has increased dramatically over the last few decades. Healthcare planners and managers regularly reference quality measurement as the key to providing the necessary assurance to doctors, patients and the public that the best quality of service is being achieved within available resources[1]. Quality assurance is a basic idea involving the setting of standards for a service, followed by delivery of the service to meet the standards consistently[2].

Obtaining robust measurements of quality in healthcare relies entirely on the provision of data that are reliable, valid, complete and meaningful. The reality is that the collection of data for quality measurement in busy clinical settings is extremely difficult. There is also a widespread lack of confidence in presently available hospital information systems because they are too often designed around financial and administrative requirements and do not adequately meet clinical needs[3]. These issues formed the backdrop to the development of the Myocardial Infarction National Audit Project (MINAP) whose aim is to carry out a national audit of the standards of care in acute myocardial infarction (AMI) as outlined by the national service framework (NSF) for coronary heart disease[4].

This chapter will outline some of the key considerations that underlie the development of MINAP, beginning with the establishment of the core data set and then describing the methods undertaken to put together robust data collection regimens and promote clinical confidence in the data.

The need for data quality

In 1979, the Merrison Royal Commission proclaimed that the information available within the NHS left much to be desired, was produced too late to assist decisions, and was often of dubious accuracy[5]. Major efforts have been made to remedy the situation[6] but the 1979 indictment of

NHS information systems still rings true among a broad layer of clinicians and healthcare planners. In 1996, Hopkins expressed the frustration of many when he commented that unless an item of information needs to be collected for some aspect of management or for billing purposes, it is highly unlikely that it will be collected routinely[7].

There is also considerable concern about the accuracy of presently available hospital data based on clinical codes derived from the World Health Organization International Classification of Diseases (ICD) 10th revision[8]. A study by Norris involving experienced cardiac care unit nurses has revealed substantial disparities between clinical coding results and those arrived at by use of strict inclusion/exclusion criteria[9]. The ICD system serves a role in providing health statistics according to a set of definitions that are not necessarily applicable in all settings. As in most situations, tools have to be designed to suit a purpose – hence the choice of classification must be determined by the interest of the investigator using the statistics that have been compiled[8].

In 1998, the Clinical Effectiveness and Evaluation Unit of the Royal College of Physicians (RCP) of London established a steering group comprising a broad representation of organisations including the British Cardiac Society (BCS), the British Heart Foundation, the Faculty of Public Health Medicine, the Department of Health, the NHS Executive, and representatives from healthcare management, nursing and the ambulance service. The steering group noted that, unless clinicians share some involvement in the processes of collecting and analysing data, it is unlikely that either the profession or management will feel sufficiently confident of any conclusions drawn from them[10].

Addressing issues of data quality

The development of a core data set, with agreed terms and definitions, is essential for the collection of comparable data[11].

The steering group developed the AMI core data set to examine the process of management and outcome of AMI. Data items were determined by the NSF requirements, established evidence and experience from previous audits or research projects. They were based on a set of principles that data items must be relevant, of valid clinical significance, limited to the agreed minimum, with priority given to ease of data capture. They should also be clearly and unambiguously defined, collected as close to the patient and the time of treatment as possible, and thus integrated into the routine patient management process[10].

A core data set is designed to be collected continuously, and thus needs to be regularly reviewed and appropriately developed in the light of experience and future advances. This is critical to ensuring confidence in the validity and relevance of the data collected.

The national audit project is based on a collaboration with the Central Cardiac Audit Database (CCAD) (discussed in Chapter 9). CCAD provides a mechanism of data transmission according to stringent data security measures that follow principles of data security and confidentiality laid down by Anderson in his review commissioned by the British Medical Association[12].

This process allows hospitals to view their own data in comparison to the aggregate of all participating hospitals. It enables clinicians to validate and use their data immediately as well as feeding back comments regarding the presentation of the data. Confidence in the quality of these data is essential to the credibility of their analysis and thus to their acceptance by all who use the data.

Evaluating data quality by means of a trial study

A trial study of the MI core data set was carried out in nine sites with the aim of identifying and measuring aspects of data quality:

■ content validity

■ feasibility

■ accuracy, and

■ reliability.

The trial study sought to identify key issues requiring further development prior to implementation of the core data set nationally.

The core data set implementation and data collection were closely monitored in each of the sites as outlined in Table 1. All comments, questions and reports were separately documented and categorised on a database according to which core data set field(s) they referred and to what type of quality issue(s) they were linked. The key messages and developments resulting from the analysis of these feedback data, and experience gained from conducting the trial study, resulted in the developments discussed below.

Implementation of data collection in hospitals

The methods used are illustrated in Fig 1. With the staff and facilities available, it is impossible to arrange site visits to all hospitals, so there needs to be a dialogue with a lead person at each hospital who is a member of the team caring for patients with MI. This person must in turn liaise with cardiologists and physicians, and with clinical audit and

Table 1. Procedures for the nine trial sites.

Site visits and meetings	Where possible CEEU and all key persons involved (representatives from the cardiology team, A&E, clinical audit, IT, ambulance, cardiac rehabilitation and pharmacy) were invited to attend an initial structured site visit. This was dominated by discussions regarding practicalities of local core data set implementation and collection. Other in-house meetings and subsequent site visits were conducted where necessary.
Audit diaries	The use of diaries by all those involved in data collection was encouraged. The importance of documenting ALL their experiences was emphasised. The diary included text describing the purpose of the diary, how the information would be used, and listing prompt questions regarding data quality.
Telephone hot line/ e-mails/faxes/reports	The telephone hot line and fax numbers were clearly stated in the information packs and diaries, and all participants were encouraged to use them.
Central monitoring	There were periodic semi-structured telephone interviews to document progress and ensure continuous communication between CEEU and trial sites.
Workshop	The workshop aimed to discuss issues identified from the feedback, and to provide an opportunity for the trial sites to present experiences and recommendations. Representation from those involved in clinical, technical and operational aspects of the audit was encouraged. One representative from each site was asked to present on the data collection process adopted at his or her hospital.

A&E = accident and emergency; CEEU = Clinical Effectiveness and Evaluation Unit; IT = information technology.

information technology (IT) departments at the hospital. Others who may need to be involved are:

- pharmacy departments, for recording take-home drugs
- rehabilitation nurses, who may be able to identify patients not admitted to coronary care
- accident and emergency (A&E) departments, for details of thrombolytic treatment given in A&E and for data on patients who die before they can be admitted to hospital
- pathology departments, for details of raised cardiac enzymes or markers which might identify patients who would otherwise be missed, and
- resuscitation officers, for data on resuscitations from cardiac arrest.

Contact must be made with CCAD, a dedicated computer made available and software installed. The last two are the responsibility of the

Fig 1. Methods used in the implementation of data collection in hospitals (A&E = accident and emergency; CCAD = Central Cardiac Audit Database; CEEU = Clinical Effectiveness and Evaluation Unit; ID = identification; IT = information technology; MINAP = Myocardial Infarction National Audit Project; PC = personal computer; rehab = rehabilitation; resus = resuscitation).

hospital's IT department. Finally, staff must be trained, responsibilities allocated, and systems put in place for ensuring and monitoring data quality.

Feedback and dialogue with the Clinical Effectiveness and Evaluation Unit

Procedures to ensure that appropriate developments are made in the light of continuous feedback and experience are carried out by using a help desk whose tasks are summarised in a flow chart (Fig 2).

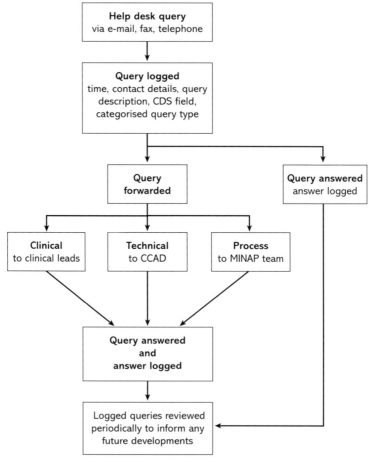

Fig 2. Flow chart summarising the functions of the help desk (CCAD = Central Cardiac Audit Database; CDS = core data set; MINAP = Myocardial Infarction National Audit Project).

Changes which have been made as a result of this process may be summarised:

▮ The contents of the core data set were changed by the addition of one field and a number of additional options to other fields.

▮ Methods to limit the burden of data collection were promoted, including the recommendation to collect secondary prevention, test and intervention data as a cyclical audit to be carried out for three months in every 12-month period.

▮ Clarification of which patients to include, data entry in different clinical situations and definitions of the core data set fields and options were further elucidated by additional context sensitive help in the MINAP software and comprehensive explanations in the help manuals provided.

▮ Recommendation that at least 5% of the data entered on the data application should be validated against the clinical notes until the proposed development and implementation of more rigorous data quality guidelines.

Establishing systems to ensure quality

The MINAP software has data validation procedures at the time of data entry using an algorithm to check the validity of the NHS number and produces initial data quality reports locally. It provides the opportunity to correct and complete data even after it has been transmitted to CCAD as the most current export overwrites previous data. This mechanism lists patients for whom there are:

▮ missing or invalid dates, times and diagnoses

▮ missing or invalid demographic data

▮ extreme or invalid date/time/delay values

▮ possible duplicate records.

MINAP is planning to undertake a data quality study in collaboration with the London regional pharmacists, the British Association of Accident and Emergency Medicine, the Ambulance Service Association and the NHS Information Authority (NHSIA). The study will retrospectively review one month's data in at least 10 sites to assess the completeness of both case identification and data entry, and the accuracy and reliability of the data. Accurate case identification is crucial to determine the denominators for the number of thrombolysis eligible patients (NSF Standard 6) and the total number of MI patients who receive secondary prevention (NSF Standard 7). Comparisons will be made between data submitted to CCAD and case notes and other data sources (eg pathology, pharmacy, clinical coding and A&E records). The study will issue a report based on an evaluation of the current standard of data quality, and produce a monitoring framework to help ensure the quality of the national audit data.

The NHSIA has developed a data accreditation scheme[13] designed to look at the timeliness, completeness, validity and accuracy of trust data. The protocols and recommendations from the MINAP data quality study will be designed to integrate into this data accreditation scheme.

How should the data be used?

Clinicians will have access to the analysis of data from their own hospital and to the aggregated data, but not to data from other individual hospitals. However, there are others who will have an interest in analyses from both individual hospitals and the aggregated data. The Commission for Health Improvement and regional offices of the NHS Executive will use national indicators to judge performance of individual organisations. At regional level, analysis will assess the relative performance of individual health authorities, ambulance services and hospital trusts to monitor progress of NSF targets and allow comparison of the organisation of care in different hospitals. At health authority and primary care trust level, data analysis can identify problems in access to and delivery of effective and appropriate care. Trust chief executives will require data relating to clinical governance and the NSF. Data analysis will also be of interest to patients and carers as a reflection of local health performance against national standards.

The national audit project has sought to outline some of the determinants for providing good quality analyses that can be of use throughout the health service. Some of the considerations for applying data derived measures to monitor healthcare are listed in Table 2[14–16].

Workshop recommendations

As part of the process of establishing a robust format for quality analysis, the project held a workshop discussion early in 2001 involving a multidisciplinary team of clinicians, health managers and planners to discuss criteria for providing analyses. The workshop underscored the importance of establishing robust data validation systems, including validation of case selection criteria, to ensure accuracy, reliability and completeness. Hospitals whose data are poor should be excluded from any analysis and may require external audit. The workshop also stated

Table 2. Some considerations in applying data derived measures to monitor healthcare.

Validity	Ensuring that any measurement criteria are accurate and actually measure what they intend to measure.
Accuracy and reliability	Ensuring there is reliability, repeatability and internal consistency behind any analyses presented.
Responsiveness or sensitivity to change	The ability to detect and measure clinically important changes.
Applicability and interpretability	Involving pragmatic issues like the feasibility of collecting the required data, the meaningfulness of the data to respondents, together with attention to confounding variables like case-mix and data quality.

that data should be presented to different audiences in such a way that they can easily interpret them. Some of the key benchmarks will be:

- delays to thrombolytic treatment
- the proportion of eligible patients who are treated, and
- the numbers of successful resuscitations.

The workshop also recommended that publication of outcome data such as mortality is deferred until the number of cases is large enough and data quality has been established.

Summary

The purpose of MINAP is to provide contemporary high quality data analyses to monitor the required NSF standards for the treatment of MI. It also allows clinicians to compare the performance of their units with others. Good data validation is vitally important in such comparative audit in which performance locally and nationally is compared. The confidence of everyone involved ultimately depends upon the integrity of data recording and analysis. Previous audits have offered total anonymity to collaborators, but it is unlikely that in future this degree of confidentiality will be possible – or even necessary. If clinicians are satisfied with the quality of the data, there is little to be gained from anonymity.

MINAP has encouraged clinicians to be involved from the outset of the project, to ensure that data collection is designed to serve their clinical needs and to develop a sense of ownership. This is encouraged by the facility to view their own results live online in comparison with pooled national data. Modifications to both the core data set and MINAP software have resulted from feedback from clinicians. Although data quality is ultimately the responsibility of hospital chief executives, clinical ownership is vital to establish quality.

Data for the purpose of audit should be collected with the same rigour and attention to accuracy as might be expected in research. MINAP does not aim to derive new knowledge about what is best practice or how to change practice. This does not, however, rule out the possibility that a large collection of data could provide valuable insights and generate hypotheses for further research. Professor Sir George Alberti (President, RCP) and Dr Howard Swanton (President, BCS) have stated that:

> *while analyses based on data of doubtful quality breed cynicism and frustration within the service, good quality data can provide a powerful engine for change and improvement[10].*

References

1   Department of Health. *Working for patients.* London: HMSO, 1989.

2   Ellis R, Whittington D. *Quality assurance in health care – a handbook.* London: Edward Arnold, 1993.

3   Wyatt JC. Hospital information management: the need for clinical leadership. *Br Med J* 1995;**311**:175–8.

4   Department of Health. *National service framework for coronary heart disease: modern standards and service models.* London: DoH, 2000.

5   Windsor P. *Introducing Korner.* Surrey: *British Journal of Healthcare* Computing Books, 1986.

6   Steering Group on Health Services Information. *Report on the collection and use of information about hospital clinical activity in the National Health Service.* London: HMSO, 1982.

7   Hopkins A. Clinical audit: time for a reappraisal? Review. *J R Coll Physicians Lond* 1996;**30**:415–25.

8   *International Statistical Classification of Diseases and Related Health Problems,* 10th revision, vol 2. Geneva: World Health Organization, 1993.

9   Norris RM. A new performance indicator for acute myocardial infarction. *Heart* 2001;**85**:395–401.

10 Birkhead JS, Norris R, Quinn T, Pearson M. *Acute myocardial infarction: a core data set for monitoring standards of care.* London: Royal College of Physicians, 1999.

11 Birkhead J. Minimum data sets for angina: a necessary basis for audit. In: de Bono D, Hopkins A (eds). *Management of stable angina.* London: Royal College of Physicians, 1994:133–43.

12 Anderson R. Clinical system security: interim guidelines. *Br Med J* 1996;**312**: 109–11.

13 *Data accreditation for acute providers,* version 2. Document Ref No. 2000–1A–328. London: NHS Information Authority, August 2000.

14 Streiner DL, Norman GR. *Health measurement scales: a practical guide to their development and use.* Oxford: Oxford University Press, 1989.

15 Long A. Assessing health and social outcomes. In: Popay J, Williams G (eds). *Researching the people's health.* London: Routledge, 1994.

16 Pearson MG, Bucknall CE. *Measuring clinical outcome in asthma.* London: Royal College of Physicians, 1999.

13 | Lessons from two previous audits of myocardial infarction

Robin Norris

The most important objective of the Myocardial Infarction National Audit Project (MINAP) is to provide feedback to clinicians about how their acute coronary services are performing and how performance might be improved. Data must be credible and statistically meaningful. This chapter discusses some major obstacles to achieving these aims, and suggests some possible, at least partial, solutions. Illustrative data come from two studies:

1 The UK Heart Attack Study (UKHAS)[1-3], carried out in the health districts of Brighton, South Glamorgan and York during 1994–95.

2 The Southern Heart Attack Response Project (SHARP)[4], performed in four South Coast hospitals during 1997–99.

This chapter will first discuss case ascertainment and recording, and the problems of definition and case mix as possible confounders for the use of case fatality as a performance indicator. A possible solution (which will be discussed later) is to look at the reverse of case fatality as an alternative performance indicator: that is, lives saved per 1,000 cases treated.

There are three major problems in achieving a successful audit:

1 Case ascertainment and recording.

2 The definition of acute myocardial infarction (AMI).

3 Case mix.

Case ascertainment and recording

Examination of the MINAP database shows that about 75% of the data should be obtainable on admission or soon after admission to the coronary care unit (CCU). We hope that this will be seen by the nursing and junior medical staff as a stage towards development of the electronic patient record, and by the nurses as an alternative to writing lengthy nursing notes.

The problems are the remaining 25% of data: the take-home drugs, invasive investigations and, in many cases, the final diagnosis and outcome. Also, how are data from non-coronary care patients to be recorded, and can this realistically be achieved given the staff time available? It seems essential that one person, preferably a senior CCU nurse, be given dedicated time to oversee the project. He or she would need back-up from clinical audit and pharmacy, and also from rehabilitation or cardiac liaison nurses – if the hospital has them – for identification of non-CCU cases.

Definition of acute myocardial infarction

UKHAS and SHARP used the 'two out of three' criteria, namely, a typical or compatible clinical history, sequential ECG changes, and a rise in serum enzyme activity to at least twice the upper limit of normal for the hospital laboratory.

There are problems with each of these criteria: not all patients with infarction experience chest pain, diabetics and some patients with inferior infarction in particular present with symptoms which are compatible rather than typical, sequential ST and T wave changes occur in unstable angina, and creatine kinase (CK) activity is raised after trauma and intramuscular injections.

However, the flexibility which is allowed by the 'two out of three' criteria makes definition reasonably robust under most circumstances.

Disparities between methods of diagnosis

After completion of the SHARP study we examined the clinical coding diagnoses of all 640 cases recorded at one of the participating hospitals. This was done to illustrate the disparities between clinical diagnoses based on the 'two out of three' criteria and diagnoses recorded by clinical coding using the International Classification of Diseases 10 definitions. A first coding diagnosis of AMI had not been given to 135 of the 640 cases, while a further 71 had been coded as infarction but had been rejected by the study, although in nearly all cases the notes had been scrutinised. This gave a 79% sensitivity of clinical coding for identification of study cases and a positive predictive value for coding of 88%.

The coding diagnoses of the 135 cases which had been accepted as AMI by the SHARP study but not by the clinical coding department are shown in Table 1. The major confounder was unstable angina which accounted for about half of these cases. Another important group was 'cardiac arrest'. The cases coded as infarction but rejected by the study included infarcts in patients already hospitalised (which our study had excluded) and patients with a convincing history but who did not fulfil the strict 'two out of three' criteria.

Table 1. Hospital coded diagnosis of 640 study patients[4].

Coded diagnosis	No. of patients
Acute myocardial infarction	505
Unstable angina	64
Other angina	8
Myocardial infarction as second code	6
Angina as second code	3
Chronic IHD	8
Cardiac arrest	11
Cardiac failure	7
Arrhythmia	8
Aortic aneurysm	2
Cardiomyopathy	1
Pericarditis	1
Non-cardiac diagnosis	5
Records could not matched*	11
Total	*640*

* Includes one patient who died in accident and emergency and had no hospital number.
IHD = ischaemic heart disease.

Clearly, there are major problems in relying on clinical coding diagnoses for definition of MINAP cases. Unless guidelines for clinical coding departments can be reconciled with definitions used by MINAP (based essentially on the 'two out of three' criteria), entry of 'final diagnosis' on the database should be performed at each hospital by the person whose job it is to oversee the project, ideally with reference to a consultant physician in doubtful cases.

Redefinition of acute myocardial infarction using troponin levels

A more recent, but equally difficult, problem is the proposed redefinition of AMI by use of troponin T or troponin I levels as a serum marker[5]. In summary, the diagnostic criteria suggested by an expert panel are 'a typical rise and gradual fall (troponin) or more rapid rise and fall (CK-MB) of biochemical markers of necrosis', together with at least one of four other defined criteria. This was said to be a consensus document, but the redefinition has been challenged by at least one committee member[6] on the grounds that it, first, ignores fatal cases (where death occurs before the marker can be measured or becomes elevated) and, secondly, includes minor elevations such as occur following coronary angioplasty, which should be properly termed 'myocardial injury'.

A survey of English hospital facilities carried out during mid-2000[7] showed that 50% of hospitals measured troponin T or I whereas 91% measured CK. Since this survey was performed, however, it appears that many hospitals are abandoning CK measurement in favour of troponin. Should this occur, the major problem for MINAP is that many cases formerly classified as unstable angina will be diagnosed as MI using the new criteria. Troponin T is raised in at least 30% of cases of unstable angina[8,9] and unstable angina is now more common in hospitals than acute infarction (UKHAS; unpublished data). Thus, there is the possibility that the reported population of infarcts from a given hospital could be diluted by up to 50% by cases which would previously have been diagnosed as unstable angina or as a single episode of acute myocardial ischaemia. Consequently, case fatality may be diluted to an unpredictable degree. Adjustments have been made to the MINAP database in order to determine:

▌ which serum marker is being used at a particular hospital

▌ the upper range of normal for the hospital laboratory, and

▌ the highest recorded level for each patient.

The challenge will remain as to how to analyse and compare data so that clinicians can be properly appraised of their own performance in comparison with that of the average for the rest of the country.

Case mix

Age

Given these difficulties in definition, what about the problem of case mix? The single most important prognostic factor in AMI is age. In UKHAS, age accounted for a greater than fivefold difference in case fatality between ages below 55 and 65–74 years (Fig 1). Had we studied patients older than 74 years, fatality would have been even higher and the number of cases would probably have increased by about 40%[10,11]. Case fatality rates in AMI are meaningless unless they are age stratified or age adjusted.

Myocardial damage

The second most important prognostic factor is the severity of myocardial damage, judged most easily by the presence or absence of left ventricular failure. Using a simple clinical definition of cardiac failure in UKHAS, one-third of patients had cardiac failure and their fatality rate was tenfold

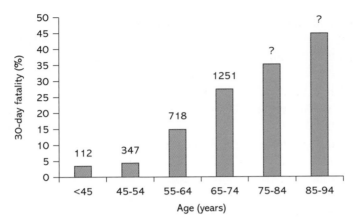

Fig 1. Case fatality rates as recorded by the UK Heart Attack Study[2] for age groups from below 45 to 65–74 years. Rates for 75–84 years and 85–94 years are speculative, but are similar to UK published figures[11].

higher than those without failure (Fig 2). Interestingly, because of the large numbers, the 99% confidence limits of the 33% with heart failure were only ±2%. Given reasonably large numbers of cases from a given hospital, variations in case mix due to differences in severity of infarction should not unduly confound comparisons.

Circumstances in which the infarct occurs

A much less widely appreciated potential confounder of case fatality rates, although I believe equally important for the MINAP project, is the

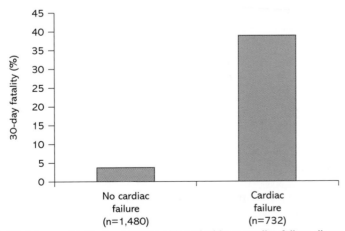

Fig 2. 30-day case fatality for patients with and without cardiac failure diagnosed using standard clinical criteria[2].

circumstances of occurrence of the infarct. If we had included in UKHAS only those patients who were admitted with AMI and who had not had a pre-hospital cardiac arrest, the 30-day fatality would have been 14%. However, the fatality rate in the substantial minority of patients who did not present in this way was much higher:

- those arriving with an unassisted cardiac output after an out-of-hospital arrest: 50% fatality
- those whose infarct started whilst they were in hospital for another reason: 45%, and
- those who had an unexpected cardiac arrest, but attributed retrospectively to coronary heart disease (CHD), while they were in hospital for another reason: 96%.

In addition, a few patients presented moribund to the accident and emergency departments. If all these groups had been included, case fatality would have increased by nearly 50% (from 14% to 20%) (Table 2).

For the purposes of the MINAP project, I believe that we should exclude infarcts and arrests in hospital and also patients who die before they have an ECG. On the other hand, patients who arrive with an unassisted cardiac output after an out-of-hospital arrest should be included.

Given all these pitfalls of definition and case mix, we can perhaps start to understand the widely divergent figures for case fatality produced by the government in 1999[12]. Table 3 shows the figures for 30-day fatality for patients over 50 years of age in the four 'best' and the four 'worst' large acute hospitals. The figures vary more than threefold from the best, 5,388 per 100,000 (5.4%), to the worst, 16,573 per 100,000 (16.6%). The last figure shown in Table 3 is a nonsense. The interpretation of these divergences must surely be that they have little to do with varying standards of care and everything to do with varying practices in clinical

Table 2. Circumstances of hospitalised acute myocardial infarction (AMI) (2,428 patients admitted to four hospitals), UKHAS 1994–95[3].

Circumstance	Patients (% of 2,428)	30-day fatality (%)	Cumulative fatality (%)
Admitted with AMI; no OOH arrest	86	14	14
Admitted after OOH arrest	5	50	16
AMI while already in hospital	5	45	17
Cardiac arrest in hospital	3	96	19
Arrived moribund; no ECG taken	1	100	20

OOH = out-of-hospital.

Table 3. How the NHS performs: deaths in hospital within 30 days of emergency admission with a heart attack[12].

Death rate per 100,000 (England)	Reported	Possible lowest	Possible highest
NHS hospital type/large acute			
Royal Shrewsbury Hospitals	5,388	2,823	7,953
Stockport Acute Services	6,271	4,179	8,362
Stoke Mandeville Hospital	6,470	3,760	6,251
Queen Mary's Sidcup	6,686	3,797	9,575
Luton & Dunstable Hospital	15,294	11,332	19,257
Sandwell Healthcare	16,567	11,760	21,374
Mid-Cheshire Hospitals	16,573	11,449	21,697
Royal United Hospitals Bath	20,000	0	20,000

coding and variable case mix – in particular, the age structure of the populations served by the different hospitals.

The approach of the Myocardial Infarction National Audit Project to these problems

How can MINAP deal with these problems?

1 If we are to use case fatality as a performance indicator we must come to grips with the problem of clinical coding. At least initially, I believe each case will have to be categorised individually using the 'two out of three' criteria.

2 Case fatality must be age stratified or age adjusted.

3 The analysis should be restricted to events starting outside hospital, including out-of-hospital arrests.

Two problems remain:

1 A major problem is that extra resources are needed for identification of patients not admitted to coronary care.

2 An unresolved problem is the possible use of different serum markers by different hospitals.

Lives saved as an alternative to case fatality

A possible, at least partial, solution to the above problems is, in a sense, to stand the analysis on its head and talk about *success* rather than *failure*, using lives saved per 1,000 patients treated as a performance indicator[4]. This concept is commonly used in meta-analyses of clinical trials and can also be used to measure performance. If we accept that resuscitation from cardiac arrest and thrombolytic therapy are the only two treatments of proven efficacy during the acute phase of MI, each patient successfully resuscitated and discharged from hospital can be counted as a life saved. Clinical trial data can be used to estimate lives saved by thrombolysis. The estimate by the Fibrinolytic Therapy Trialists (FTT) reported in 1994[13] was of 30 lives saved per 1,000 patients presenting with ST elevation or bundle branch block and treated within six hours of onset. This estimate was later revised by Boersma and colleagues[14] to include the concept of the 'golden hour', so that patients treated within one hour of onset had about double the advantage. After the first hour, salvage estimated by Boersma was not significantly different from that estimated by the FTT collaborators.

Unfortunately, the Boersma concept does not seem to be relevant to patients presently treated with thrombolysis in UK hospitals; we found an identical proportion of only 2% treated within one hour of onset of symptoms in both the UKHAS and SHARP studies[2,4]. The formula for calculating lives saved per 1,000 cases treated is:

(*n* successfully resuscitated x 1,000/*n* treated) + (proportion given thrombolytic therapy x 30)

An example over a two-year period from four district general hospitals is shown in Fig 3.

There are two caveats to the use of 30 lives saved per 1,000 treated as a measure of the efficacy of thrombolytic treatment:

1 It does not acknowledge the life-saving antithrombotic effect of aspirin, which was found in the International Study of Infarct Survival-2 trial[15] to be similar in degree to that of streptokinase (about 24 lives saved per 1,000 treated). The use of aspirin is now near universal, however, so inclusion of an extra term for its use is unlikely to differentiate good from poor performance in MINAP.

2 The criterion of 30 per 1,000 saved applies only to treatment in hospital with streptokinase. If restoration of flow to the infarct related artery could be established more quickly than at present by pre-hospital treatment either with a more rapid plasminogen activator given within the 'golden hour' or by primary angioplasty performed immediately after arrival at hospital, 30 lives saved would be an underestimate and the term for thrombolysis would need to be modified[14]. Until this happens, 30 per 1,000 is the best estimate we have[13].

Given the present practice of administration of streptokinase in hospital, variations in call-to-needle or door-to-needle times are unlikely

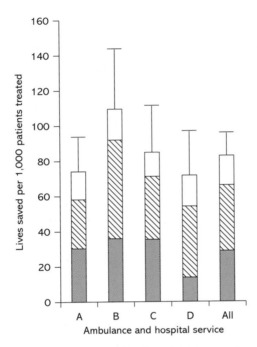

Fig 3. Lives saved per 1,000 patients treated at four district general hospitals 1997–99 (black = lives saved by resuscitation from out-of-hospital cardiac arrest by ambulance personnel; hatched = lives saved by resuscitation in hospital; clear = lives estimated to have been saved by thrombolytic treatment). Note that 80% of salvage was attributable to resuscitation, and about 40% of successful resuscitations were performed outside hospital by the ambulance service (reproduced, with permission, from Ref 4).

to change the estimate of 30 per 1,000 appreciably, despite the importance of these as a measure of hospital staff performance and the importance attached to them by the national service framework for CHD[16]. The MINAP database has the potential to discover more important variations in standards of care as far as prevention of deaths from AMI is concerned (ie variations in success of resuscitation from cardiac arrest) than variations in delay for administration of thrombolytic therapy (Fig 3).

Non-coronary care cases

A recurring problem in planning MINAP is what to do about non-CCU cases. Identification and documentation of these might demand more resources than are available in many hospitals. It is also possible that use of lives saved rather than case fatality as a performance indicator might make the analysis more robust. Even in hospitals in which a large proportion of cases of MI cannot be admitted to CCU because of shortage of beds, nearly all patients with cardiac arrest or who have been given thrombolytic treatment are admitted and so can be easily identified and counted. This does not solve the problem of the denominator, the total number of patients treated; this would need to be established independently, preferably by an alternative method to clinical coding as currently practised.

Summary

Experience from previous audits suggests that case ascertainment and recording requires half to one day per week of dedicated time from somebody, ideally a CCU nurse. This person needs back-up from other hospital departments, particularly audit and of course information technology. This is particularly important if all cases of MI, not just CCU cases, are to be included. Definitions in particular, and to a lesser degree case mix, are real confounders and are no doubt the principal reasons for the widely divergent figures for case fatality reported not only in the 1999 government survey[12] but also in the literature[10,11,17]. The new definition of MI[5] can only make matters worse.

A possible solution is to look at lives saved as an alternative to case fatality as a performance indicator. Successful resuscitation and thrombolytic treatment are easily recorded, and uncertainties with definition will have a lesser effect because they appear in the denominator of the expression rather than in the numerator: that is, the 1,000 patients treated and not the lives saved.

References

1 Norris RM. Fatality outside hospital from acute coronary events in three British health districts, 1994–5. The United Kingdom Heart Attack Study Collaborative Group. *Br Med J* 1998;**316**:1065–70.

2 Effect of time from onset to coming under care on fatality of patients with acute myocardial infarction: effect of resuscitation and thrombolytic treatment. The United Kingdom Heart Attack Study (UKHAS) Collaborative Group. *Heart* 1998;**80**:114–20.

3 Norris RM (on behalf of the UK Heart Attack Study investigators). Sudden cardiac death and acute myocardial infarction in three British Health Districts: the UK Heart Attack Study. London: British Heart Foundation, 1999.

4 Norris RM. A new performance indicator for acute myocardial infarction. *Heart* 2001;**85**:395–401.

5 Myocardial infarction redefined – a consensus document of The Joint European Society of Cardiology/American College of Cardiology Committee for the redefinition of myocardial infarction. Review. *Eur Heart J* 2000;**21**: 1502–13.

6   Tunstall-Pedoe H. Comment on the ESC/ACC redefinition of myocardial infarction by a consensus dissenter. *Eur Heart J* 2001;**22**:613–5.

7   Birkhead J. A baseline survey of facilities for the management of acute myocardial infarction in England 2000. London: Royal College of Physicians, 2001.

8   Hamm CW, Ravkilde J, Gerhardt W, Jorgensen P, *et al.* The prognostic value of serum troponin T in unstable angina. *N Engl J Med* 1992;**327**:146–50.

9   Stubbs P, Collinson P, Moseley D, Greenwood T, Noble M. Prospective study of the role of cardiac troponin T in patients admitted with unstable angina. *Br Med J* 1996;**313**:262–4.

10 Maynard C, Weaver WD, Litwin PE, Martin JS, *et al.* Hospital mortality in acute myocardial infarction in the era of reperfusion therapy (the Myocardial Infarction Triage and Intervention Project). *Am J Cardiol* 1993;**72**:877–82.

11 Brown N, Young T, Gray D, Skene AM, Hampton JR. Inpatient deaths from acute myocardial infarction, 1982–92: analysis of data in the Nottingham heart attack register. *Br Med J* 1997;**315**:159–64.

12 *The Times*, June 17, 1999.

13 Indications for fibrinolytic therapy in suspected acute myocardial infarction: collaborative overview of early mortality and major morbidity results from all randomised trials of more than 1000 patients. Review. Fibrinolytic Therapy Trialists' (FTT) Collaborative Group. *Lancet* 1994;**343**:311–22.

14 Boersma E, Maas AC, Deckers JW, Simoons ML. Early thrombolytic treatment in acute myocardial infarction: reappraisal of the golden hour. *Lancet* 1996; **348**:771–5.

15 Randomised trial of intravenous streptokinase, oral aspirin, both, or neither among 17,187 cases of suspected acute myocardial infarction: ISIS-2. ISIS-2 (Second International Study of Infarct Survival) Collaborative Group. *Lancet* 1988;**ii**:349–60.

16 Department of Health. *National service framework for coronary heart disease: modern standards and service models.* London: DoH, 2000.

17 Rogers WJ, Bowlby LJ, Chandra NC, French WJ, *et al.* Treatment of myocardial infarction in the United States (1990 to 1993). Observations from the National Registry of Myocardial Infarction. *Circulation* 1994;**90**:2103–14.

14 Future developments in audit of the acute ischaemic syndromes

Raphael Balcon

Clinical data collection has traditionally been performed by individuals or small groups using diverse systems, which means that the information frequently cannot be integrated with other sources of data. This greatly limits the credibility of the data and their ultimate value. The concept of a national database with clearly defined variables, collecting and collating information from many centres, is not new but has rarely been achieved.

The Myocardial Infarction National Audit Project

The Myocardial Infarction National Audit Project (MINAP) was a response to a government initiative to provide a framework for the NHS, clearly stating aims and deliverables. Coronary heart disease (CHD) was one of the first national service frameworks to be implemented, and myocardial infarction (MI) was chosen to initiate the project because it is an easily defined and recognised entity. The Central Cardiac Audit Database (CCAD) team was an obvious choice to deal with data collection and analysis as it had already established an embryo national cardiac database in a pilot study.

The essence of such a national database is that it enables all outcomes to be evaluated once the patient has entered the system, not just the outcome of a particular event seen in isolation. Two critical requirements need to be fulfilled to achieve this satisfactorily, both of which have been attained by CCAD:

1 Full mortality reporting.
2 Record linking.

Full mortality reporting

It is possible to achieve full mortality reporting by linking to the death registry of the Office for National Statistics (ONS). The experience in the CCAD pilot study has been revealing, in that 30-day mortality reported by centres for various interventions has generally been considerably less than the true number reported by ONS. There are many reasons for this, some unavoidable, for instance when the death has occurred out of

123

hospital. Some hospital deaths, however, have not been recorded, perhaps because the patient was transferred to the care of a different specialist or to another hospital not contributing to CCAD. The experience clearly confirms the need for independent and reliable mortality reporting.

Record linking

The second requirement is record linking by use of the NHS number. This means that patients can be tracked wherever they appear in the hospital system, provided that the hospital is contributing data to CCAD. This is not dependent on the NHS net, since the software used by CCAD has a high level of data protection using a double encryption technique, and secure transmission is possible over the internet. Some data protection and communication issues remain to be resolved before full record linkage becomes possible. In the future, data from general practice could be included if the electronic patient record becomes a reality.

At present, a relatively small proportion of patients with MI are routinely investigated and have interventions in the acute phase, despite good evidence that primary angioplasty with stent implantation (PCI) has better results than standard therapy[1,2]. The main reason for this is the lack of facilities and manpower to implement such a strategy, and the financial implications of doing so. Patients with continuing symptoms, however, are usually transferred to cardiac centres where they undergo angiography and often then proceed to PCI or coronary surgery. These patients represent as many as 50% of the interventions carried out in most cardiac centres. All these outcome data are missed in the absence of record linkage and universal contribution to a national database. The problem would be compounded if primary PCI were to be used more frequently.

Data

From the practical point of view, the MINAP data form part of the existing CCAD database created during the CCAD pilot. The data are divided into various types including, for instance:

- demographic
- coronary intervention
- coronary surgery, and
- myocardial infarction.

The records are created locally and then imported into a CCAD 'feeder' database; from there, they are imported into the CCAD main patient database starting with the demographic information. If the patient already exists, the new information is added to the existing record, in the central national database. These processes are all automated.

Infrastructure

The infrastructure required to handle the MINAP data is the same as that needed for the whole CCAD system, so that the existing coronary angiography, percutaneous intervention and coronary surgery modules will be available to centres equipped to carry out these procedures. A number of cardiac centres do not treat patients in the acute phase of MI – and therefore will not automatically be included in the project – but deal with patients if they have recurrent symptoms in hospital. These centres would need to contribute to CCAD for the MINAP database to include the interventional outcomes so that all the data could be integrated chronologically. For the first time, the outcome for patients rather than for isolated procedures would be available.

Other acute coronary syndromes

It is intended to tackle the other acute coronary syndromes next. Coronary angiography and intervention, where appropriate, are the rule, and outcome evaluation without these data would be impossible. The planned extension of MINAP to all district general hospitals – where most patients with acute coronary syndromes are admitted – would mean that their information can easily be captured. Only inclusion of the cardiac centres without acute coronary care would be needed to ensure completeness of the data.

The resulting database would become extremely powerful in following the outcomes of procedures and events experienced by patients with coronary disease, even more so if the information is included from chest pain clinics currently being set up.

Use and abuse of information

It is important that such powerful information is not abused. In particular, medical professionals should be reassured that it will not be used for political purposes, but only for monitoring and improving patient care. In order to achieve this, there must be agreed methods of evaluating outcomes and performance.

Effect of case mix

There has been a great deal of discussion about the effect of case mix on outcomes of procedures. Many believe that it is too complex to evaluate; it has been suggested that it is best to define 'index' cases that are agreed to be straightforward, and for which an acceptable range of performance and outcome can be agreed. These problems need resolution, and are being addressed now.

The current situation

MINAP has helped set the standard for data collection for the purposes of monitoring provision of service, performance and outcomes. The MI element of the project has been successfully launched, and the early experience has been good. At the time of writing, 230 of the 235 hospitals in England and Wales treating AMI have enrolled, 183 have started data collection, and information has been collected on more than 18,000 patients. The potential for a comprehensive national CHD database can be realised if there are appropriate mechanisms to control the use of the data by all those rightfully concerned with the project, so that all centres conscientiously enter information.

References

1   Stone GW, Grines CL, Browne KF, Marco J, *et al.* Outcome of different reperfusion strategies in patients with former contraindications to thrombolytic therapy: a comparison of primary angioplasty and tissue plasminogen activator. Primary Angioplasty in Myocardial Infarction (PAMI) Investigators. *Cathet Cardiovasc Diagn* 1996;**39**:333–9.

2   Grines CL, Cox DA, Stone GW, Garcia E, *et al.* Coronary angioplasty with or without stent implantation for acute myocardial infarction. Stent Primary Angioplasty in Myocardial Infarction Study Group. *N Engl J Med* 1999;**341**: 1949–56.

Glossary

A&E	accident and emergency
ACEI	angiotensin-converting enzyme inhibitor
(A)MI	(acute) myocardial infarction
ASANCEP	Ambulance Services Association National Clinical Effectiveness Programme
BCS	British Cardiac Society
CCAD	Central Cardiac Audit Database
CCU	coronary care unit
CEEU	Clinical Effectiveness and Evaluation Unit
CFR	case fatality rate
CHD	coronary heart disease
CHI	Commission for Health Improvement
CI	confidence interval
CK	creatine kinase
CSB	Clinical Standards Board (Scotland)
DoH	Department of Health
GP	general practitioner
HES	hospital episode statistics
HOI	hospital outcome indicator
ICD	International Classification of Diseases
IHD	ischaemic heart disease
ISD	Information and Statistics Division
ISIS	International Study of Infarct Survival
IT	information technology
JRCALC	Joint Royal Colleges Ambulance Liaison Committee
LV	left ventricular
MINAP	Myocardial Infarction National Audit Project
MONICA	Monitoring Trends and Determinants in Cardiovascular Disease
NAOMI	National Audit of Myocardial Infarction
NCA	needs care assessment
NCHOD	National Centre for Health Outcomes Development
NHSIA	NHS Information Authority
NICE	National Institute for Clinical Excellence
NSF	national service framework
ONS	Office for National Statistics
OR	odds ratio
ORLS	Oxford Record Linkage System
PAS	patient administration system
PCI	primary angioplasty with stent implantation
RCP	Royal College of Physicians

SEACAG	South-East Ambulance Clinical Audit Group
SHARP	Southern Heart Attack Response Project
SMR	(i) standardised mortality ratio
	(ii) Scottish Morbidity Record
SPSS	Statistical Package for the Social Sciences
UKHAS	UK Heart Attack Study
WHO	World Health Organization